OXFORD BUSINESS ENGLISH SKILLS

Effective

PRESENTATIONS

JEREMY COMFORT

with YORK ASSOCIATES

OXFORD UNIVERSITY PRESS

Oxford University Press
Great Clarendon Street, Oxford OX2 6DP

Oxford New York
Athens Auckland Bangkok Bogotá Buenos Aires
Calcutta Cape Town Chennai Dar es Salaam
Delhi Florence Hong Kong Istanbul Karachi
Kuala Lumpur Madrid Melbourne Mexico City
Mumbai Nairobi Paris São Paulo Shanghai
Singapore Taipei Tokyo Toronto Warsaw

and associated companies in
Berlin Ibadan

Oxford and *Oxford English*
are trade marks of Oxford University Press

ISBN 0 19 457065 7
© Oxford University Press

First published 1995
Fifth impression 2001

No unauthorized photocopying

Acknowledgements

Illustrations by Nigel Paige
Photography by Mike Hertz
Cover illustration by Adam Willis

The publishers would like to thank the
following for permission to reproduce
photographs:

Art Directors
Cephas Picture Library
Robert Harding Picture Library
The Image Bank
NIKE (UK) Ltd
Oxford Picture Library
Science Photo Library
Tony Stone Images

Typeset Franklin Gothic
and Adobe Minion

Printed in Hong Kong

Contents

Introduction

For learners of Business English, making a presentation in English can be difficult and demanding. The presenter needs certain skills which go beyond the range of ordinary language courses. *Effective Presentations* is a practical course which develops these skills. It can be used as a short, intensive specialist course, or integrated into a longer and more general Business English programme. It takes the learner systematically through the key stages of making presentations, from planning and introducing to concluding and handling questions. However, each unit can also be used separately to focus on particular elements of giving presentations. By the end of their period of study, learners should be able to make clear, well-organized presentations in front of an audience.

Course components

The course consists of four components: a video, a student's book, an audio cassette, and a teacher's book.

The video

The video, which lasts approximately 35 minutes, is central to the course. It contains extracts from four different presentations of the kind that most professional people need to make. The video acts as the focus for all the activities contained in the student's book.

The student's book

The book consists of nine units, which correspond to those in the video. Each unit is divided into three sections: communication skills, language knowledge, and presentation practice.

The communication skills section focuses on the key presentation skills demonstrated in the video. The language knowledge section looks at useful language for performing these skills. The presentation practice section allows the learner to put both communication skills and language knowledge into practice using realistic tasks, and their own ideas and experience.

The audio cassette

The audio cassette provides additional presentation extracts and listening activities, which illustrate key language points.

The teacher's book

This book contains handling notes for the teacher, and includes extra, photocopiable presentation practice material.

The approach

Effective Presentations looks first at some of the important things that presenters often get wrong, before demonstrating ways of avoiding these mistakes. For this reason, the video provides both bad models and good models for students to analyze and consider. It then breaks down a presentation into its important stages, concentrating on two main areas.

Communication skills

The video demonstrates skills such as structuring information, using an appropriate style of language, using visual aids, and adopting the right body language. These are then analyzed and practised with the support of the student's book.

Language knowledge

The student's book presents language areas such as the use of linkers and connectors, referring to graphs and charts, emphasizing and minimizing information, and the contrast between written and spoken language. These are further demonstrated by extracts and exercises on audio cassette.

Using the course

The course is designed to work either as classroom or self-study material.

In the classroom

At the start of the course, the learners should each make a short presentation on a familiar topic. If possible, this should be recorded on video. The learners will receive feedback from the teacher. This should identify the skills which need improving. Depending on the learners' needs, the course can either be followed from start to finish, or focus on selected units, using the good and bad models in the video and the activities in the student's book. At the end of the course, the learners should repeat their initial presentation (or give a different one), incorporating the skills and language shown in the good models. This version can also be video recorded and compared with their first presentation.

Self-study

Effective Presentations can be used successfully for independent self-study. The student's book provides comprehensive viewing and follow-up activities. These are designed to guide the learners through the course and help them to evaluate their own performance. Self-study can also be integrated into a classroom-based course. The language knowledge section of each unit in the student's book includes exercises which could be done as self-study tasks, and then followed up in the next class. Similarly, it is particularly useful for learners to prepare for the presentation practice phase in self-study time, as this will avoid using up valuable classroom time.

1 What is the point?

Objectives

Communication skills	**to identify what makes a presentation effective**
Language knowledge	**time expressions and tenses**
Presentation practice	**to practise presenting background information**

Communication skills

Pre-viewing

1 What makes a good presentation? List all the things you think make a good presentation. Compare your list with the key on page 57.

2 Read the Video Presentation Context. Imagine you are making the presentation.

a What content will you include?

b How will you structure the content?

Video Presentation Context

The company	The presenter	The audience	The presentation

The company

Westwood Brewery, based in London, is a traditional company. It has recently created the post of Public Relations (PR) Manager in order to improve the company's image in the market.

The presenter

Joanna Brookes is Westwood's new PR Manager. One of the first things she does is to organize a meeting to discuss the brewery's corporate image – in particular whether it needs to be changed.

The audience

Joanna has invited the senior managers of the brewery and some outside consultants. They are expecting to participate in a meeting about the corporate image of the brewery.

The presentation

Unfortunately, Joanna gets the date wrong. She only realizes her mistake when her secretary tells her that the audience is waiting in the conference room. She starts the meeting with a short presentation. The presentation should introduce the main topics for discussion.

Viewing

▶ 3 Watch the video from 00.00 to 03.18. As you watch, note down what Joanna does *badly*. Use this checklist to help you. Compare your notes with the key on pages 57–8.

Checklist

Overall
- [ ] Does she consider the audience?
- [ ] Does she have clear objectives (to inform, to amuse, to persuade, to train)?

System
- [ ] Is her presentation well prepared?
- [ ] Is there a clear structure (beginning, middle, end)?
- [ ] Does she link the parts together?
- [ ] Is the content relevant and interesting?
- [ ] Has she considered the timing?

Delivery
- [ ] Does she speak clearly?
- [ ] Does she speak at the right speed?
- [ ] Does she use appropriate language?

Body language
- [ ] Does she use her body to emphasize meaning?
- [ ] Does she maintain eye contact with the audience?
- [ ] Does she appear confident and positive?

Visual aids
- [ ] Are the visual aids clear?
- [ ] Do they support her message?
- [ ] Does she use the equipment professionally?

Other comments

▶ 4 Watch the video again from 00.00 to 03.18. This time, make brief notes on the content of Joanna's presentation. What points does she make?

Post-viewing

5 One of the worst things about Joanna's presentation is its lack of organization. Look at the 'classic' presentation structure below and your notes from Viewing 4.

a What should Joanna include in her presentation?
b How should she organize it?

Introduction	→	Outline	→	Main parts	→	Summary	→	Conclusion
				1				
				2				
				3				

Language knowledge

JOANNA BROOKES
'*Of course, we were a family firm...*'

1 You are going to hear Westwood's Peter Blake presenting some background information on his company. The information falls into three time zones and Peter uses a combination of time expressions and verb tenses to indicate these.

A	B	C	Key
The company was bought in 1982.	We've had some difficult years recently.	We employ 250 in the plant.	**A** Finished time **B** Unfinished time **C** Present time

As you listen, complete these extracts. Then decide which time zone each extract falls into. The first two have been done for you. Check your answers in the key on page 58.

a As you all know, the brewery was bought *back in 1982.* (A)

b ...as I'm sure you're all aware, there've been some major changes *since that date.* (B)

c _____, the new owners announced a new strategy for growth. (__)

d ...in fact, _____ it has dropped further... (__)

e ...it _____ stands at just 180, nearly 20% less than ten years ago. (__)

f _____, we have invested heavily in new plant and equipment. (__)

g As an indication, _____ we spent nearly £1 million on new vats. (__)

h It may surprise you to know that _____ Westwood had no marketing department. (__)

i _____, we recruited Pamela Taylor as Marketing Manager... (__)

j ...and _____ she has built her department into a major force in the company. (__)

Language focus Time expressions and tenses

Past time

some time ago
last year
in the past
back in 1978

The past simple

The past simple is used to indicate finished time:
She joined the company in 1994.

Regular verbs form the past simple by adding *-ed* to the verb stem.
The *-ed* ending can be pronounced in three different ways:
/t/ *announced*   /ɪd/ *started*   /d/ *ordered*

Irregular verbs form the past simple in a number of ways. It sometimes helps to group them by sound:
buy – bought   catch – caught   teach – taught

Recent time

over the last few years
recently
since 1992

The present perfect

The present perfect is used when the time is unfinished or not stated.
It is formed with *have/has* + the past participle:
He has resigned.
They have retired.

The auxiliary *have/has* is usually contracted in spoken English:
'*He's just started.*'
'*They've already left.*'

Present time

currently
at the moment
now
at present

The present simple

The present simple is used to report on current status:
It currently stands at 180.
He is retired now.

Don't forget to pronounce the *-s* in the third person:
It stands.
He lives.

2   Complete these sentences. Use the time expression to help you choose the correct tense of the verb: past simple, present perfect, or present simple. Check your answers in the key on page 58.

a Some time ago, we ———— (sell) the company.

b Recently, we ———— (invest) a lot in new equipment.

c The current head count ———— (stand) at 280.

d Since last year, we ———— (increase) our PR budget.

e In 1985, he ———— (retire) from the company.

3   Complete these sentences. Use the tense of the verbs to choose the correct time expression from the list below. Check your answers in the key on page 58.

back in the eighties   last month
over the last few years   since January
at the moment

a _____, we used to have much bigger expense accounts.

b _____, our output stands at 150 per hour.

c He has been with us _____.

d _____ production dropped to 140 per hour.

e _____, we have dramatically increased productivity.

Pair work

4   Listen to this short dialogue, paying particular attention to the contracted verb forms. Then, with a partner, practise saying the dialogue naturally.

A: When did you get back?
B: Just last night.
A: So how long've you been away?
B: Nearly two weeks.
A: Lucky devil! I haven't had a holiday in ages.
B: That's not true. You're always going away.
A: But that's on business.
B: So you say! It sounds fun to me. You know, first-class hotels and all that.
A: You should try it. It's more stressful than you might think.

5   Change the extract from a presentation into more natural spoken English by using contractions. Check your answer in the key on page 58.

I would have liked to speak for longer on this subject, but I am afraid I have not got enough time. However, I would like to say a few words about future prospects. This year, we have had some major problems; next year, we will face even more severe ones. This is certain, as the market is becoming more competitive.

Presentation practice

1 Use the information below to prepare and give a short presentation on the history of Sonway Solar Electronics.

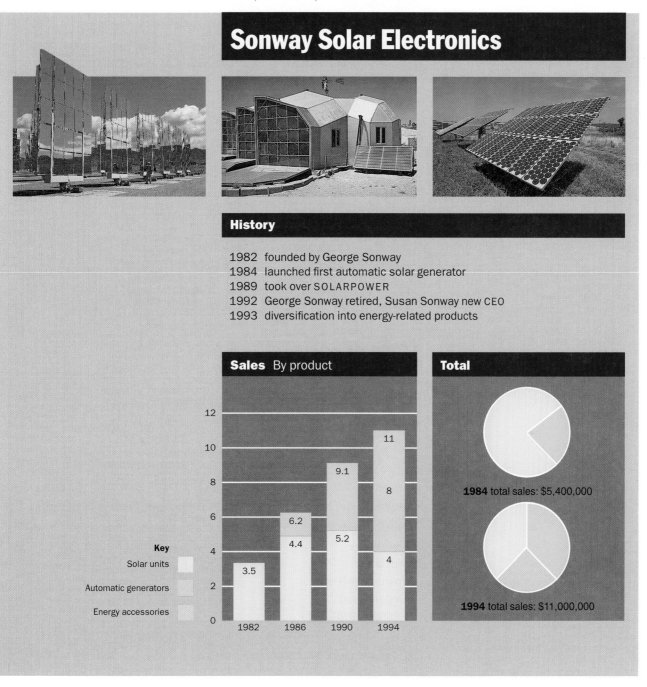

Sonway Solar Electronics

History

1982 founded by George Sonway
1984 launched first automatic solar generator
1989 took over SOLARPOWER
1992 George Sonway retired, Susan Sonway new CEO
1993 diversification into energy-related products

Sales By product

Key
Solar units
Automatic generators
Energy accessories

1982: 3.5
1986: 6.2, 4.4
1990: 9.1, 5.2
1994: 11, 8, 4

Total

1984 total sales: $5,400,000

1994 total sales: $11,000,000

2 Prepare and present some background information on one of the following:

a your own company's history
b a product history
c your career so far
d a subject of your choice.

2 Making a start

Objectives

Communication skills	to identify what makes a good introduction to a presentation
Language knowledge	introducing yourself and your talk
Presentation practice	to practise giving the introduction to a presentation

Communication skills

Pre-viewing

1 Which of the items on the checklist below would you include in the introduction to:

a an internal presentation to colleagues?
b an internal presentation to bosses?
c an external presentation to customers?
d an external presentation to suppliers?

> ### Checklist
>
> - your name and position
> - the title/subject of your presentation
> - the purpose of your presentation
> - the length of time you will take
> - the main parts or points you will cover
> - any visual aids you will use
> - when the audience may ask questions
> - a reference to the audience: a human touch

2 How would you introduce yourself at the beginning of a presentation? Which of these would you include?

First name
Surname
Position/job title
Department
Job responsibilities

Practise putting them together to produce a fluent introduction of yourself.

3 Read the Video Presentation Context. Imagine you are making the presentation. What will you include in the introduction?

Video Presentation Context

The company	The presenter	The audience	The presentation

Standard Electronics is an innovative high-tech electronics company. It regularly runs tours around the plant.	Normally, the tours are led by Sarah Peters, a Marketing Assistant. Unfortunately, she is ill, so Geoff Maxwell, the Factory Manager, has been asked to stand in for her.	Some business people are arriving at Standard Electronics for a tour of the plant. Before the tour, there will be a presentation about the company.	The presentation should give an overview of the company's activities. We see Geoff Maxwell in two moods. In Version 1, he is annoyed that he has been asked to run the tour. In Version 2, he is prepared to do a professional job.

Viewing

▶ 4   Watch Version 1 of the video from 03.29 to 04.30. Which items in the checklist in Pre-viewing 1 does Geoff include in his introduction? Note down any points you notice about his presentation. Compare your notes with the key on page 59.

▶ 5   Watch Version 2 of the video from 04.30 to 06.00. Which items in the checklist does Geoff include this time? Note down anything you particularly like about his introduction. Compare your notes with the key on page 59.

▶ 6   Watch Version 2 again from 04.30 to 06.00. Stop the video each time Geoff mentions one of the items in the checklist.

Post-viewing

7   Choose a presentation you have already given, and prepare and give the introduction.

Language knowledge

GEOFF MAXWELL
'Hello and welcome to Standard Electronics. I'm Geoff Maxwell, the Factory Manager in charge of the plant you'll be seeing today.'

Language focus   Introducing yourself and your talk

Greeting, name, position

Good morning. My name's (…). I'm the new Finance Manager.

Ladies and gentlemen. It's an honour to have the opportunity to address such a distinguished audience.

Good morning. Let me start by saying just a few words about my own background. I started out in …

Welcome to Standard Electronics. I know I've met some of you, but just for the benefit of those I haven't, my name's (…).

Title/Subject

I'd like to talk (to you) today about …

I'm going to | *present the recent …*
explain our position on …
brief you on …
inform you about …
describe …

The | *subject* | *of my* | *talk*
focus | *presentation*
topic | *paper (academic)*
speech (usually to public audience)

Purpose/Objective

We are here today to | *decide …*
agree …
learn about …

The purpose of this talk is to | *update you on …*
put you in the picture about …
give you the background to …

This talk is designed to | *act as a springboard for discussion.*
start the ball rolling.

Length

I shall only take (…) minutes of your time.
I plan to be brief.
This should only last (…) minutes.

Outline/Main parts

I've divided my presentation into four parts/sections. They are …

The subject can be looked at under the following headings: …

We can break this area down into the following fields:
Firstly/first of all …
Secondly/then/next …
Thirdly/and then we come to …
Finally/lastly/last of all …

Questions

I'd be glad to answer any questions at the end of my talk.
If you have any questions, please feel free to interrupt.
Please interrupt me if there's something which needs clarifying. Otherwise, there'll be time for discussion at the end.

Reference to the audience

I can see many of you are …
I know you've all travelled a long way.
You all look as though you've heard this before.

1 You are going to hear twelve extracts from the introductions to two presentations — one internal, one external. As you listen, decide which presentation each extract comes from and complete the table. The first one has been done for you. Check your answers in the key on page 59.

Presentation	Extract
Internal: to colleagues at a budget meeting	*a*
External: to delegates at a professional conference	

2 Complete this presentation introduction with words from the list. Check your answers in the key on page 59.

talk about	look at	points of view
questions	brief	finally
hear	act as	go along

Good afternoon and thank you for making the effort to be here with us today. My name's Rachel Rawlins and I'm responsible for public affairs. What I'd like to do today is ^a_____ our recent corporate campaign. This ^b_____ talk will hopefully ^c_____ a springboard for discussion. I'm going to ^d_____ the corporate campaign from three ^e_____: firstly, the customers; secondly, the financial institutions; and ^f_____, the shareholders. If you have any ^g_____, just interrupt me as I ^h_____. Your point of view may well be different, and we'd like to ⁱ_____ from you.

3 Complete these sentences. Choose the correct verb. The first one has been done for you. Check your answers in the key on page 59.

a I'd like to *inform* you of the latest news.
1 speak   2 inform   3 describe

b Could you _____ up? We can't hear you at the back.
1 talk   2 say   3 speak

c I'll have to _____ the place as I don't have any photographs with me.
1 explain   2 describe   3 present

d He's going to _____ the latest results.
1 describe   2 inform   3 present

e Let me _____ why we need to cut costs.
1 explain   2 describe   3 talk

f We'll have time to _____ about this over lunch.
1 discuss   2 say   3 talk

g I couldn't _____ how long will it take.
1 talk   2 speak   3 say

h We will _____ you when the project comes to an end.
1 say   2 describe   3 tell

4 Introductions can become repetitive. It's important to have a choice of words and expressions at your fingertips.

Use one of the following expressions to replace each of the expressions in italics in this introduction. Check your answers in the key on page 59.

don't hesitate	a chance	I take care
I'm delighted	sections	go through
in more depth	my purpose is	divide

> Good morning, ladies and gentlemen. *It's a pleasure* [a] to be with you today. My name's Gordon Matthews and *I'm in charge* [b] of corporate finance at our headquarters here in Brussels. *We are here today* [c] to *review* [d] some key figures and to outline financial strategy over the next five years. So what I intend to do is to *break down* [e] this presentation into three *parts* [f]: first, the financial review; second, the options facing us; and finally, the strategy I propose. If you have any questions, please *feel free* [g] to interrupt me, but I should also say there'll be *an opportunity* [h] to discuss issues *at greater length* [i] after my talk.

Presentation practice

1 Prepare and give the introduction to these presentations.

	a	b	c	d
Audience	Company employees	Visitors	Colleagues	Boss

Subject	Salary freeze:
	  –reasons
	  –implementation
		Company overview	Change in organization	Your salary increase

Purpose	To inform	To describe	To discuss	To persuade
Time	10 minutes	20 minutes	5 minutes	1 minute!

2 Choose a presentation you have given recently or are preparing to give. Prepare and give the introduction.

3 Linking the parts

Objectives

Communication skills	**to identify ways of organizing a presentation**
Language knowledge	**key words and phrases for linking ideas**
Presentation practice	**to practise signposting the organization of a presentation**

Communication skills

Pre-viewing

1 Look at these different ways of organizing information and ideas.

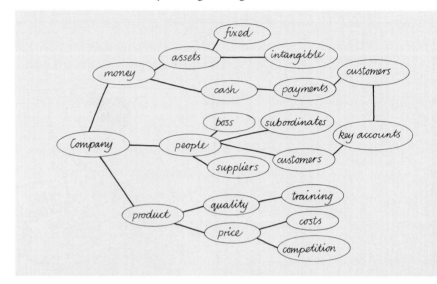

1 PEOPLE	–bosses
	–subordinates
2 MONEY	–assets
	–cash
3 PRODUCTS	–quality
	–price

people	**money**	**products**
bosses	assets	quality
subordinates	cash	price
customers		
suppliers		

2 Choose one of the following topics and brainstorm your ideas on it, using one of the methods in 1 above to organize your ideas:

  Methods of communication
  The life cycle of a company
  Business in the 21st century

3 Read the Video Presentation Context. Imagine you are making the presentation about your company.

  a What content will you include?
  b How will you organize the content?

Video Presentation Context

The company	The presenter	The audience	The presentation

Standard Electronics is an innovative high-tech electronics company. It regularly runs tours around the plant.	Normally, the tours are led by Sarah Peters, a Marketing Assistant. Unfortunately, she is ill, so Geoff Maxwell, the Factory Manager, has been asked to stand in for her.	Some business people are arriving at Standard Electronics for a tour of the plant. Before the tour, there will be a presentation about the company.	The presentation should give an overview of the company's activities. It should be divided into three or four clear parts. We see Geoff Maxwell in two moods. In Version 1, he is annoyed that he has been asked to run the tour. In Version 2, he is prepared to do a professional job.

Viewing

▶ 4 Watch Version 1 of the video from 06.12 to 07.23. As you watch, make notes on the content and organization of Geoff's talk. Compare your notes with the key on page 59.

▶ 5 Watch Version 2 of the video from 07.24 to 09.40. As you watch, complete Geoff's presentation notes. Check your answers in the key on page 59.

Point 1:

Point 2: *Main markets (and Manton news story)*

Point 3:

Post-viewing

6 In Version 2 of his presentation, Geoff follows this approach:

This technique has two advantages: it's easier for the audience to follow the presentation, and it's easier for the speaker to follow his or her plan.

Look back at the notes you made on Pre-viewing 2 and practise using this approach to present your key points.

Language knowledge

GEOFF MAXWELL
'And that brings me to the final part
of this short introduction.'

1   The items on the left are extracts from Geoff's presentation. Match each
    one with a sentence on the right which means the same. The first one has
    been done for you. Check your answers in the key on page 59.

    a   OK, let's start with the history.

    b   Anyway, I'll leave the history
        there.

    c   So, let's turn now to a brief
        overview of our main markets.

    d   By the way, you may have seen
        the story in the news.

    e   Anyway, let me get back to what I
        was saying about new markets.

    f   And that brings me to the final
        part of this short introduction.

    g   So, before I go on, are there any
        questions?

    1   In passing, let me tell you about a
        press report.

    2   So, we come to the last part of my
        introduction.

    3   To start with the history then.

    4   That covers the history.

    5   To come back to the point I was
        making.

    6   Let's stop here and see if there are
        any questions.

    7   So, we can go on to a survey of
        our principal markets.

2   You are going to hear six extracts from another presentation about cutting
    costs. The speaker uses a variety of words and phrases to link the points he
    is making. As you listen, identify the linked ideas. The first one has been
    done for you. Check your answers in the key on page 59.

    a   cutting costs
    b   healthy margins
    c   not the only ones
    d   point-of-sale competition
    e   launch new packet size
    f   initiatives have failed

    1   raise sales in major outlets
    2   no change in sales
    3   losing money
    4   competitor has closed plant
    5   over-hasty reactions
    6   aggressive discounting

Language focus Linking ideas

Sequencing/Ordering

firstly… secondly… thirdly…
then… next… finally/lastly…
let's start with…
let's move/go on to…
now we come to…
that brings us to…
let's leave that…
that covers…
let's get back to…

Giving reasons/causes

therefore
so
as a result
that's why

Contrasting

but
however

Comparing

similarly
in the same way

Contradicting

in fact
actually

Summarizing

to sum up
in brief
in short

Concluding

in conclusion
to conclude

Highlighting

in particular
especially

Digressing

by the way
in passing

Giving examples

for example
for instance
such as

Generalizing

usually
generally
as a rule

---

3 Link the ideas in these sentences by adding an appropriate word or phrase. Compare your answers with the key on page 60.

a That was a good meeting. (*By the way…*)
Did I tell you about the match last night?

b Our competitors are becoming stronger.
One of them, Falcon, has a joint venture with a Japanese firm.

c I've divided this into two parts.
The issue of profit-sharing.
The question of share option schemes.

d This year we have lost market share.
We expect to remain No. 1 in the market.

e There are some vital factors to consider.
The risk of a take-over bid.

f Falcon has reduced its costs by relocating.
We must consider cutting the cost of our premises.

g We've had a difficult year.
We've still made a healthy profit.

h We expected to lose money in the Far East.
This was our most profitable market.

i The yen dropped against the dollar.
We made considerable profits on the exchange rate.

j There have been some failures on occasions.
We have been very successful.

Presentation practice

1   Use the information below to prepare and give two short presentations.
    Practise linking your points and ideas clearly.

a   Learning styles

> Four types of learner
> activist
> pragmatist
> theorist
> reflector
> Activists
>   learn by doing, not thinking about doing
>   activity is the key
> Pragmatists
>   learn when they can see the point
>   objectives are the key
> Theorists
>   learn when they can understand the underlying system
>   systems and categories are the key
> Reflectors
>   learn when they have a chance to reflect in their own time
>   time to think is the key

b   Training for business

```
Types of training:
technical
management

technical training
information technology (computers)
objective: to keep a technical edge over the
   competition
training for efficiency
   (e.g. production methods)

versus
training for innovation
   (e.g. new technology)
95% of employees receive some technical
   training

management training
leadership/team management/strategy
objective: to run an efficient business
3% of employees receive management training
```

2 Prepare and give a presentation on a subject of your choice. Use this flow-chart to help you.

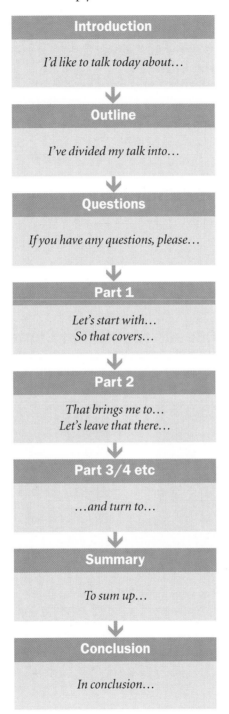

Introduction

I'd like to talk today about…

Outline

I've divided my talk into…

Questions

If you have any questions, please…

Part 1

Let's start with…
So that covers…

Part 2

That brings me to…
Let's leave that there…

Part 3/4 etc

…and turn to…

Summary

To sum up…

Conclusion

In conclusion…

4 The right kind of language

Objectives

Communication skills	**to show the advantages of speaking rather than reading a presentation**
Language knowledge	**personal and impersonal styles of language**
Presentation practice	**to practise changing written language into spoken language**

Communication skills

Pre-viewing

1   What's wrong with reading a presentation? List the advantages and disadvantages of reading presentations. Compare your list with the key on page 60.

2   Read the Video Presentation Context.

Video Presentation Context

The organization

The Association of International Management (AIM) is holding its annual conference. As usual, the conference programme includes presentations on a wide variety of subjects.

The presenter

Dr Linden is well known for his publications in the field of management psychology. At the AIM conference, he is presenting a paper on 'Leadership styles'.

The audience

All members of the audience are involved in management (e.g. personnel, training, and development) and have chosen this presentation from the information in the programme.

The presentation

Dr Linden will report on the results of recent surveys into leadership styles and career promotion prospects. These surveys are based on corporate interviews carried out world-wide.

Viewing

▶ **3** Watch Versions 1 and 2 of the video from 09.49 to 15.25. As you watch, make notes on Dr Linden's presentation. Use this checklist to help you. Compare your notes with the key on page 60.

Checklist

	Version 1	Version 2
Eye contact		
Language complexity?		
sentence length?		
use of pauses?		
(im)personal?		
Manner open or closed?		
(un)interested?		

Post-viewing

4 Which version of Dr Linden's presentation is easier to understand? Read the instructions below and, using the video transcripts on page 75 and page 76, calculate the Fog Index for both versions of his presentation.

The Fog Index

The Fog Index (invented by Robert Gunning) is a mathematical formula for measuring the comprehensibility of language (usually written language).

$$F = 0.4 \, (A + L)$$

Key

F = Fog Index
A = the average length of sentences
L = the number of long words per 100 words (a long word has three or more syllables excluding the endings -ed, -es, -ing)

Language knowledge

DR LINDEN [Version 1]
'Next slide. In the American part of the survey it was found that…'

DR LINDEN [Version 2]
'We can see in this next slide the results from the American part of the survey.'

1 Look at the differences between written and spoken language. Then read the extracts from Dr Linden's presentations, a-d below, and decide which are written language and which are spoken language. Find examples in each extract to support your answers. Check your answers in the key on page 61.

Written language	Spoken language
long sentences	shorter sentences
complex vocabulary	simpler vocabulary
complex arguments	simpler arguments
impersonal style	personal style

a You can see here, 35% of the group of managers classified as participative reached senior management positions. On the other hand, 74% of the more individualistic managers achieved senior management status.

b An individualistic style appears to be closely associated with rapid career path progression, whereas a group or participative style, despite its evident attractiveness to all members of staff, is correlated with a relatively slow career progression.

c Although lip service is paid to the concept of participative management, their real perceptions of leadership qualities completely contradict this view. It can be further seen that such surveys…

d So, we find there is a massive contradiction. Good managers are supposed to be participative – to make sure they consult and discuss. Good leaders are supposed to be strong individuals – able to make decisions on their own.

2 You are going to hear a point from another presentation, delivered in three different styles. As you listen, complete the table. Check your answers in the key on page 61.

	a	b	c
read or spoken?	———	———	———
distant or human?	———	———	———
spontaneous or prepared?	———	———	———
personal or impersonal?	———	———	———

Language focus Personal and impersonal styles

Active and passive forms

The passive is formed with the verb *to be* + the past participle. It is less personal than the active.

Tense	Active	Passive
present simple	I think	it is thought
present continuous	we are discussing	it is being discussed
present perfect	the boss has said	it has been said
past simple	John called a meeting	a meeting was called
future	I will refer to this later	this will be referred to later

Personal pronouns

Active verbs use more personal pronouns:
I think…
We are working on…

Be careful not to overuse *I. We* is a good alternative for talking about companies:
We will launch the product in June.

Reference to the audience

As I'm sure you know…
We have all experienced…
You may remember…
As I'm sure we'd all agree…

Everyday language

Using slang and everyday expressions can make an impact on the audience and add drama:
*Where's the caring side of employment gone? I'll tell you
 where. It's hiding behind a damned set of targets and
 objectives – that's where it is!*

You need to know your audience very well to use this kind of language.

---

3 Make these sentences more personal by using the active not the passive. Check your answers in the key on page 61.

a The issue of restructuring was discussed.

   We _____ .

b Money is being directed into the wrong accounts.

   The Finance Manager _____ .

c The agreement will be signed later this month.

   Both companies _____ .

d It has been found to be rather unreliable.

   I _____ .

e It is reported that shares are due to rise.

   The press _____ .

4 Make these sentences less personal by using the passive not the active. Check your answers in the key on page 61.

a I favour a reduction in working hours.

_____.

b The boss forced him to resign.

_____.

c They have transferred the money via the bank.

_____.

d We are planning an autumn sales campaign.

_____.

e Susan will reorganize the Research Department.

_____.

5 Match the more formal verbs with their less formal (spoken) equivalents. Check your answers in the key on page 61.

	formal		informal
1	to acquire	a	to put into action
2	to reduce	b	to pull out
3	to access	c	to get worse
4	to appreciate	d	to buy
5	to capture	e	to pay
6	to deteriorate	f	to cut down
7	to implement	g	to get into
8	to rationalize	h	to take
9	to remunerate	i	to understand
10	to withdraw	j	to make simpler

Presentation practice

1   Change this text into more natural spoken English. Start like this: *I'd like to talk today about...* Compare your version with the key on page 61.

Introduction

The subject of this paper is a cost-benefit analysis of introducing job sharing. The aim is to provide the necessary information for a decision to be made within the next two months. The subject will be looked at under the following headings: financial implications, working practices, and social effects.

Financial implications

A detailed study of personnel and associated costs has been carried out. From a payroll point of view, 10% of staff choosing to job share will mean no actual increase in direct salary costs. However, there will be additional costs incurred in the administration of salaries.

2   Choose a text from your own sources (e.g. a company brochure, a product description) and change it into more natural spoken language. Practise presenting the information.

5 Visual aids

Objectives

Communication skills	to show how to design and use good visual aids
Language knowledge	describing trends, charts, and graphs
Presentation practice	to practise designing and using visual aids

Communication skills

Pre-viewing

1 Look at these visuals. What do you think of them?

Design

- Attractive
- Informative
- Convenient

Product design

There are three areas that are of the utmost importance when considering the design of any new product:

1. Attracting the customer
2. Informing the customer
3. Being convenient for the customer

This is how we have dealt with these three areas:

1. The colour, shape, and texture of the bottle have been chosen after considerable research because they proved to be the ones that the pilot group considered the **most attractive**.
2. Research also showed that customers were not interested in glamorous names or the use of many colours. What they really wanted was hard information about what was inside the bottle. Once again, it was better not to use long, technical jargon to describe the contents, but to use simple language that the lay person could easily understand.
3. A surprise result was that so many of the pilot group were concerned about how easy (or difficult!) it would be to open the bottle. Many thought we had paid too much attention to safety features—making it difficult for small children to open—and not enough attention to customer convenience.

2 This checklist contains some of the 'rules' for designing and using visual aids. Discuss these rules and try to agree on some others to add to the checklist. Compare your answers with the key on page 62.

Checklist

Design

Don't use visuals to repeat what you can say with words.

Don't overcrowd visuals with too much information.

Use

Don't use too many visuals.

Don't read from the visual.

3   Read the Video Presentation Context. Imagine you are making the presentation.

   a   What sort of visuals will you use?
   b   How will you use these visuals?

Video Presentation Context

The company	The presenter	The audience	The presentation

Westwood Brewery, based in London, is a traditional company. It has recently created the post of Public Relations (PR) Manager in order to improve the company's image in the market.	Joanna Brookes is Westwood's new PR Manager. One of the first things she does is to organize a meeting to discuss the brewery's corporate image–in particular whether it needs to be changed.	Joanna has invited the senior managers of the brewery and some outside consultants. They are expecting to participate in a meeting about the corporate image of the brewery.	Unfortunately, Joanna gets the date wrong. She only realizes her mistake when her secretary tells her that the audience is waiting in the conference room. She is planning to say something about the products and the latest production figures.

Viewing

▶   4   Watch Versions 1 and 2 of the video from 15.35 to 20.30. As you watch, compare the design of Joanna's visuals. Note anything you particularly like or dislike.

▶   5   Watch Versions 1 and 2 of the video from 15.35 to 20.30 again. As you watch this time, compare the way Joanna uses her visuals. Again, note anything you particularly like or dislike.

Post-viewing

6   Design a visual (on a transparency, flip-chart, or board) on one of the following:

   a   information about your company/organization
   b   a business/management concept

Language knowledge

JOANNA BROOKES

'Production flattened out around the 480,000 mark for four years and then, more worryingly, dropped to 460,000 last year.'

1 You are going to hear Francesca Rocca, Finance Director of Marvotto, talking about turnover figures. As you listen, write the information she presents on Graph 1 below. Check your version with the key on page 62.

2 Complete this description with information from Graph 2 below. Check your answers in the key on page 62.

I'd like to draw your attention to some key figures. On this graph, I have a _____ both profitability and turnover. The b _____ line represents turnover and the c _____ one represents profits over the last ten years. As you can see, ten years ago our turnover stood at £550,000. Over the next five years it d _____ steadily. It reached a peak of £750,000 five years ago and, unfortunately, since then it has e _____. It now stands back at £550,000.

Let's look at the profit figures for a minute. During the same period, profits f _____. There was a slight g _____ in 1993, but otherwise we have h _____ our profitability throughout this period.

Graph 1

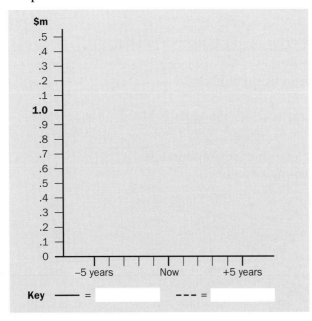

Graph 2

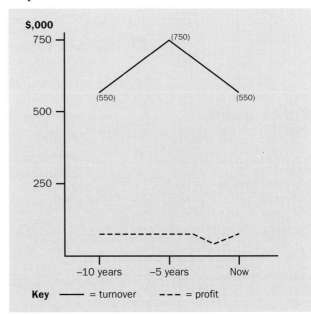

Language focus Describing trends, charts, and graphs

Types of chart

pie chart

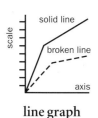

line graph

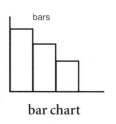

bar chart

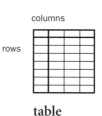

table

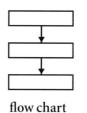

flow chart

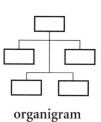

organigram

Describing change

Upward movement
to increase/rise/go up
to grow/expand
to rocket/boom

Our sales rose last year.

To increase and *to expand* can also be used transitively:
e.g. We increased sales.
  We expanded our workforce.

To raise can **only** be used transitively:
e.g. We raised our prices.

▶ **Note**
Transitive verbs can be used when we want to
express an action which affects an object.

ACTION   OBJECT
e.g. We raised our prices.

Intransitive verbs cannot be used to express an
action, only a result.

RESULT
e.g. Prices rose.

Downward movement
to decrease/fall/drop/
  decline/go down
to contract
to slump/collapse

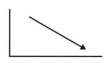

Profits have fallen recently.

To decrease and *to drop* can also be used transitively:
e.g. We have decreased our costs.
  We will drop our prices.

To reduce and *to cut* can only be used transitively:
e.g. We reduced his salary.
  We had to cut 200 jobs.

An end to movement
to flatten out/level off

Sales have flattened out.

No change
to remain constant/stable
to stay the same/at the
  same level

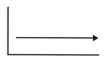

Sales have remained constant.

Three other verbs – *to maintain, to hold* and *to keep* – are
used transitively:
e.g. We plan to maintain our dividend (at the same level).
  We need to hold our costs down.
  We plan to keep our prices low.

Degree of change

dramatically/considerably/significantly/moderately/
  slightly

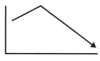

*Sales have fallen
considerably.*

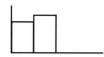

Profits rose slightly.

Speed of change

rapidly/quickly/suddenly/gradually/steadily/slowly

*Absenteeism had
dropped slowly.*

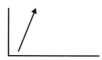

Sales went up rapidly.

3 Make these sentences transitive. The first one has been done for you. Check your answers in the key on page 62.

   a Our salaries have remained constant for five years.

     The company _____ salaries at the same level.

   b The temperature in the building has fallen.

     The caretaker _____ the temperature in the building.

   c Interest rates have risen over the last two weeks.

     Banks _____ their interest rates.

   d Production has stayed the same for some time.

     The company _____ production at the same level.

   e The average age has decreased in the company.

     Recruiting policy _____ the average age.

4 We often use noun phrases instead of verbs to describe trends. For example:

Prices *have risen considerably*.
There has been *a considerable rise* in prices.

Change the following sentences to include a noun phrase. Compare your answers with the key on page 63.

   a The market has expanded slightly.
   b Prices are going to fall dramatically.
   c Our export sales collapsed suddenly.
   d Sales are increasing steadily.
   e Salaries have dropped gradually.
   f Profits will certainly rise significantly.

'Our export sales collapsed suddenly.'

Presentation practice

1 Design and present some effective visuals on the information below.

Nike Incorporated

Foundation: 1972

Employees: 45 (1972); 6,500 (1992)

Sales: $3.2 million (1972); $3.4 billion (1992)

Share price: $5.50 (1980); $65.00 a share (1992)

1991: profit increase - 15%, sales increase - 13%

Total world-wide revenue
footwear: $2.62 billion (77%)
apparel: $628 million (18%)
other: $162 million (5%)

2 Design and present visuals to communicate the following messages.

  a An employer's desire to introduce TQM (Total Quality Management).
  b A decision to ban smoking throughout the building.
  c An announcement of a competition for the most successful sales person.

6 Body language

Objectives

Communication skills	to illustrate the importance of body language
Language knowledge	ways of emphasizing and minimizing your message
Presentation practice	to practise using language and body language to communicate your message clearly and persuasively

Communication skills

Pre-viewing

1 Use this checklist to discuss the importance of body language in presentations. Compare your ideas with the key on page 63.

Checklist

eye contact	
facial expression	
hands	
movement	
posture	

2 What body language can you use to persuade?

3 Read the Video Presentation Context.

Video Presentation Context

The organization	The presenter	The audience	The presentation

The Academic Management Institute is partly funded by local government. It is facing cuts in its budget.	Dr Linden is responsible for the budget of his department. He has called his staff together to discuss the situation. He wants to persuade them to propose an alternative.	All members of Dr Linden's staff are at the meeting. They are all worried about possible job losses.	Dr Linden intends to point out the options facing the department and the Institute.

Viewing

▶ 4 Watch Versions 1 and 2 of the video from 20.40 to 23.18 with no sound. As you watch, make notes on Dr Linden's body language. Use this checklist to help you. Compare your notes with the key on page 63.

Checklist	Version 1	Version 2
General appearance		
Stance and posture		
Hands – position		
Hands – gestures		
Eye contact		
Facial expression		
Movement		

▶ 5 Watch Version 2 of the video from 22.14 to 23.18 again, this time listening to the sound. As you watch, underline the expressions in these extracts which are strongly emphasized. The first one has been done for you. Check your answers in the key on page 64.

a These cost cuts are going to <u>cause</u> <u>considerable</u> pain.
b We need to draw up a plan of action. I have put some ideas on the board.
c These are some of the measures we could consider. There are broadly three approaches.
d First, we could accept the cuts and reduce staff drastically. Secondly, we could fight and hope to achieve some reduction in the level of the cuts. Or thirdly, and this is what I support, we could put forward an alternative proposal. Now, this would mean…

Post-viewing

6 Choose one of the topics (a-c below) and prepare a brief presentation. Try to be persuasive. (If possible, record your performance on video and use the recording for feedback. Play it back with no sound.)

a Women make better managers of people than men.
b The world is changing so fast that long-term planning is no longer feasible.
c Body language is at least as important as spoken language.

Language knowledge

DR LINDEN
'Or thirdly, and this is what I support, we could put forward an alternative proposal.'

1 You are going to hear eight short extracts from different presentations. As you listen, decide whether the language in each extract is being used to emphasize or minimize the message, and complete the table. The first one has been done for you. Check your answers in the key on page 64.

Emphasize	Minimize
	a

IT MAY COME AS A SLIGHT SUPRISE TO HEAR THAT YOU'VE BEEN PICKED TO TAKE PART IN THE COMPANY'S DOWNSIZING PROJECT.

REDUNDANCY

Language focus Emphasizing and minimizing

Emphasizing

Strong adverbs intensify adjectives:
*We've had an **extremely** good year.*

Adverbs can be total, very strong, or moderate.

TOTAL
absolutely (fantastic)
completely (awful)
entirely (depressing)

VERY STRONG
extremely (good)
very (bad)

MODERATE
fairly (safe)
reasonably (expensive)
quite (cheap)

Minimizing

Look at the way the following expressions of degree and uncertainty modify, or minimize, the message:

*It **seems** we will have to delay the delivery.*
*The Chief Executive Officer **appears** to have left the country.*

*It's **just** a little bit further.*
*We're going to reduce our staff **a bit**.*

***Perhaps** we should consider resigning.*
*There **might** be another way.*

*I **tend to** think we should stop now.*
***To some extent**, the company has failed to realize its potential.*

Intonation is also very important in giving more or less emphasis to what we say.

2　Add an adverb to these sentences to emphasize the message. Compare your answers with the key on page 64.

   a　This has been a good year. **
   b　We have had a difficult time. *
   c　We have seen a disastrous decline in our profits. ***
   d　It was easy to achieve our objectives. *
   e　The announcement was unexpected. ***
   f　I've got some bad news. **

Key

moderate *
very strong **
total ***

3　Complete these sentences with words that will minimize the message. Compare your answers with the key on page 64.

   a　We ＿＿＿＿＿＿＿＿ see things differently. ＿＿＿＿＿＿＿＿
   your experience is ＿＿＿＿＿＿＿＿ limited.

   b　＿＿＿＿＿＿＿＿, you're right. But ＿＿＿＿＿＿＿＿ we
   ＿＿＿＿＿＿＿＿ consider the long-term view.

   c　There's ＿＿＿＿＿＿＿＿ time. ＿＿＿＿＿＿＿＿ we
   ＿＿＿＿＿＿＿＿ discuss this question now.

Presentation practice

1　Change the language in this text to communicate the message more persuasively. Compare your version with the key on page 64.

> The trouble with business today is that people don't have time. Companies have reduced their workforces so that fewer people have to do the same amount of work. This means that managers don't see what is happening around them. They need their time to work through their regular tasks and have no time to take on new initiatives.
>
> Time for reflection is important. Decisions taken now not only affect today's business, they can also have an influence on business in the long term. Strategy is the concern of senior management when it needs to be the concern of everybody in the company.

2　Prepare and give a short presentation on a subject you feel strongly about. Use language, body language, and intonation to communicate your message clearly and persuasively.

7 Finishing off

Objectives

Communication skills	to identify what makes an effective ending to a presentation
Language knowledge	the language of endings
Presentation practice	to practise ending a presentation

Communication skills

Pre-viewing

1 What should go in the final part of a presentation? List the things you think should go in a presentation ending. Compare your list with the key on page 64.

2 What would you include in the endings to:

   a a farewell speech to a colleague?
   b an introduction of your department to a new colleague?

3 Read the Video Presentation Context.

Video Presentation Context

The company	The presenter	The audience	The presentation

Westwood Brewery, based in London, is a traditional company. It has recently created the post of Public Relations (PR) Manager in order to improve the company's image in the market.	Joanna Brookes is Westwood's new PR Manager. One of the first things she does is to organize a meeting to discuss the brewery's corporate image – in particular whether it needs to be changed.	Joanna has invited the senior managers of the brewery and some outside consultants. They are expecting a clear summary and a sense of direction for their discussion.	Joanna Brookes is reaching the end of her presentation. The presentation should provide a clear agenda for the discussion which follows.

Viewing

▶ 4 Watch Versions 1 and 2 of the video from 23.28 to 25.23. As you watch, note what Joanna includes in her ending each time. Compare your notes with the key on page 65.

▶ 5 Watch Version 2 from 24.24 to 25.23 again and complete Joanna's presentation notes. Check your answers in the key on page 65.

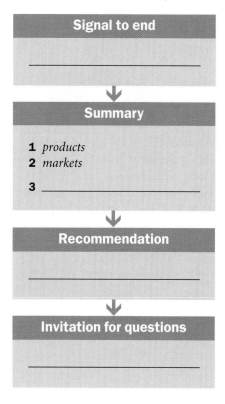

Post-viewing

6 Use the information below to prepare and give the ending of a presentation.

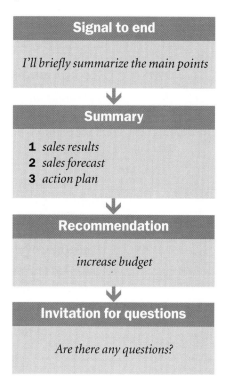

Language knowledge

JOANNA BROOKES
'So, before we move on to discuss these matters, let me just summarize the main issues. Firstly… secondly… thirdly… So, I suggest we take things in that order… Before we start, are there any questions you'd like to ask?'

1 You are going to hear the final part of four different presentations. As you listen, decide which presentation each extract comes from, and complete the table. Check your answers in the key on page 65.

Presentation	Extract
The Sales Presentation (by a salesman to a group of prospective customers)	
The Welcome Presentation (to a group of visitors to a plant)	
The New Idea Presentation (to a group of managers)	
The Motivation Presentation (by a Personnel Director to a group of new employees)	

Language focus Endings

Signalling the end

That brings me to the end of my presentation.
That completes my presentation.
Before I stop/finish, let me just say…
That covers all I wanted to say today.

Summarizing

Let me just run over the key points again.
I'll briefly summarize the main issues.
To sum up…
Briefly…

Concluding

As you can see, there are some very good reasons…
In conclusion…
I'd like to leave you with the following thought/idea.

Recommending

So, I would suggest that we…
I'd like to propose… (more formal)
In my opinion, the only way forward is…

Closing

Thank you for your attention.
Thank you for listening.
I hope you will have gained an insight into…

Inviting questions

I'd be glad to try and answer any questions.
So, let's throw it open to questions.
Any questions?

2   The sentences **a-e** below are the end of a presentation, but they are in the wrong order. Put them into the right order. Check your answer in the key on page 65.

  a   So, I'd now be glad to answer any questions.

  b   I sincerely hope you'll all go away with a more complete picture of the principal activities of UNEXCO.

  c   Very briefly, there are three. Firstly, fund-raising; secondly, publicity; and thirdly, political lobbying.

  d   So, that brings me to the end of this presentation.

  e   Finally, I'd like to leave you with something which I heard recently. 'You can't please all the people all the time, but we should certainly be able to feed all the people all the time.'

3   Make full sentences by matching the correct halves. The first one has been done for you. Check your answers in the key on page 65.

  a   Before we come to the end,   1   there are four major features.
  b   I'd be glad to answer   2   we start the discussion now.
  c   To summarize,   3   by quoting a well-known saying.
  d   We can conclude   4   we should reduce our costs.
  e   In my opinion,   5   any questions now.
  f   I'd like to suggest   6   I'd like to thank you for your participation.

Presentation practice

1   Use the information below to prepare and give the ending of a presentation on your home town.

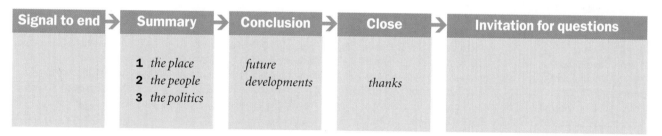

Signal to end	Summary	Conclusion	Close	Invitation for questions
	1 *the place* 2 *the people* 3 *the politics*	*future developments*	*thanks*	

2   Prepare and give the ending of a presentation on a professional subject of your choice. Include a recommendation, if appropriate.

8 Question time

Objectives

Communication skills to show how to handle questions effectively at the end of a presentation

Language knowledge asking and answering questions

Presentation practice to practise handling questions

Communication skills

Pre-viewing

1   What is the best way to handle difficult questions after a presentation? Compare your ideas with the key on page 65.

2   Read the Video Presentation Context.

Video Presentation Context

The organization	The presenter	The audience	The presentation

| |  |  |  |

The Association of International Management (AIM) is holding its annual conference. As usual, the conference programme includes presentations on a wide variety of subjects.

Dr Linden is well known for his publications in the field of management psychology. He has just finished presenting his paper on 'Leadership styles'. He awaits questions from the audience.

Three members of the audience ask Dr Linden a question. Each questioner has a different personality and style of questioning.

Dr Linden has talked about the results of recent surveys into leadership styles and career promotion prospects. These surveys are based on corporate interviews carried out world-wide.

Viewing

3   Watch Versions 1 and 2 of the video from 25.34 to 28.53, with no sound. As you watch, note the differences in body language in the two versions.

▶ 4   Watch Versions 1 and 2 from 25.34 to 28.53 again, listening to the sound. As you watch this time, note the differences in the way Dr Linden handles the questions. Mark whether he does (✓) or does not (×) carry out each stage in the checklist below. The first one has been done for you.

Checklist

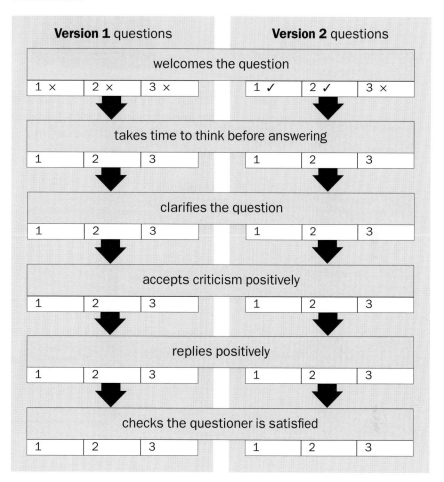

Version 1 questions			Version 2 questions		
welcomes the question			welcomes the question		
1 ×	2 ×	3 ×	1 ✓	2 ✓	3 ×
takes time to think before answering			takes time to think before answering		
1	2	3	1	2	3
clarifies the question			clarifies the question		
1	2	3	1	2	3
accepts criticism positively			accepts criticism positively		
1	2	3	1	2	3
replies positively			replies positively		
1	2	3	1	2	3
checks the questioner is satisfied			checks the questioner is satisfied		
1	2	3	1	2	3

Post-viewing

5   Work with a partner to practise handling questions. Each person should choose one of the topics (a-b below), and their partner should ask them questions about it.

a   The balance of work and home life
b   National stereotypes

Take two or three minutes to formulate and anticipate questions before you start. Use the checklist in Viewing 4 to help you. (If possible, record your performance and use the recording for feedback.)

Language knowledge

QUESTIONER
'Dr Linden? If you don't mind me asking, could you tell us how the respondents assessed difficult concepts such as individualism?'

DR LINDEN
'Of course. I suppose you're referring to the second survey I mentioned?'

1 You are going to hear Samantha O'Neill answering some questions after her presentation on product development. As you listen the first time, summarize the questions on this flow-chart. Then listen a second time and summarize her answers. Compare your answers with the key on page 65.

Questions   Answers

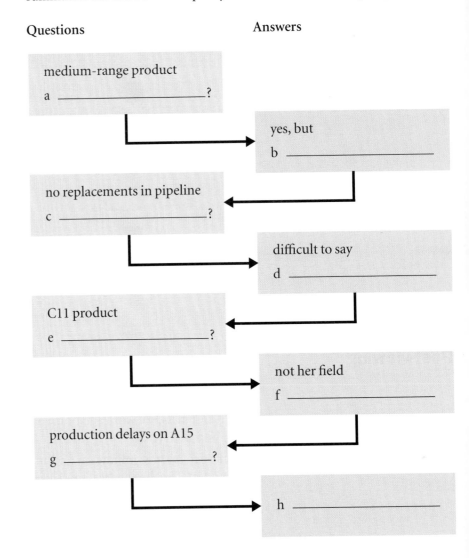

Questions	Answers
medium-range product a _____ ?	yes, but b _____
no replacements in pipeline c _____ ?	difficult to say d _____
C11 product e _____ ?	not her field f _____
production delays on A15 g _____ ?	h _____

Language focus Asking and answering questions

Direct questions

Do you have any plans for a new production plant?
Where do you plan to locate it?

Polite questions and answers

QUESTIONS

Do	you mind	if I ask you	
Would		telling me	if/whether...
			what/where/etc...
	Could/Can you tell me...		about...
	I'm interested to know...		
	I'd like to know...		

ANSWERS

Go ahead/Please do/Certainly.
That's a good question.
That's interesting.

Statement questions and answers

QUESTIONS

All the space was booked for an October launch...?
(question intonation)
It worries me that we don't have any replacements in the pipeline. Doesn't it worry you too?

ANSWERS

A positive statement question is looking for the answer 'yes':
It's going to be late, isn't it? I'm afraid so.
You've got problems with the assembly? Yes, a few.
The suppliers have done their job. Is that right? Yes, as far as I know.

A negative statement question is looking for the answer 'no':
We haven't won the contract, have we? No, it doesn't look like it.
I wasn't a success? Not much of one.
We aren't going to make it on time, are we? I'm afraid not.

If the answer contradicts the statement, the word *actually* is often used:
The plant's going to close, isn't it? Well, actually, I've just heard the company is employing more staff.

Clarifying a question

If I understand you correctly, you are saying/asking...
I didn't quite catch that.
Could you go over that again?
I'm not sure what you're getting at.

Avoiding giving an answer

Perhaps we could deal with that later.
Can we talk about that on another occasion?
I'm afraid that's not my field.
I don't have the figures with me.
I'm sure Mr (...) could answer that question.
That's interesting, but I'd prefer not to answer that today.

Checking the questioner is satisfied

Does that answer your question?
Is that clear?
May we go on?

---

 2 You are going to hear six questions. Listen and choose the best response to each question. Check your answers in the key on page 65.

a
1 No, of course not.
2 Please do.
3 No, that's a problem.

b
1 Well, actually, it's confidential.
2 Yes, I do.
3 Certainly.

c
1 You could say so.
2 That's right.
3 I'd prefer not to.

d
1 I need a break.
2 I don't need a break.
3 That's a good idea.

e
1 No, they aren't.
2 You're wrong.
3 Actually, some are at headquarters.

f
1 Any moment.
2 That's a difficult question.
3 That's interesting.

3   Put the questions and answers in these three dialogues in the correct order.
Check your answers in the key on page 66.

a

A: I'd like to ask you about next year's promotion campaign.

B: We've got a meeting next week to decide. I'll let you know straight away, if that's OK.

A: Excuse me, could I interrupt?

A: Sure, that'll be fine.

B: Sure, what exactly would you like to know?

A: Well, could you tell me at this stage whether you have fixed a budget?

B: Of course.

b

A: Would you mind telling us when you're going to retire?

B: When is it?

A: May I ask a question?

B: That sounds fine. I'll look forward to it.

B: Not at all. I'm planning to stop work just after Christmas.

A: Oh good! We'd like to invite you to our Christmas party. Can you come?

A: It's on the 24th from seven onwards.

B: Go ahead.

c

A: I see what you mean. Yes, of course we've looked at all the options and we think this is the best one.

A: Are there any questions?

A: I'm afraid that's all we have time for now. Perhaps you'd like to talk about that later.

B: Well, you know, other possibilities such as relocating to a cheaper area.

B: Yes, I wonder if you have considered any other options?

A: I'm not sure what you're getting at.

B: But surely relocation would be better for the staff?

Presentation practice

Pairwork

1   You are going to role-play a TV interview. Working with a partner, decide which role to take —interviewer or interviewee—and read your rolecard. Prepare your questions and answers before you start. (If possible, record your performance and use it for feedback.)

Interviewer

A news story has just broken. Hammond Electronics Inc. (an American multinational) is going to close its plant in Southern Germany and move to Portugal. The closure will result in more than 2,000 job losses. Your job is to interview the Human Resources Manager at Hammond's European headquarters in Brussels. Cover the following question areas:

a   reasons for relocation
b   effects of relocation
c   policy of company for European production
d   future in Germany

Interviewee

You are the Human Resources Manager at Hammond Electronics Inc. (an American multinational). You are based at the company's European headquarters in Brussels. Hammond has just announced that it will close its plant in Southern Germany and move to Portugal, with the loss of 2,000 jobs in Germany. Your job is to answer questions about this decision. Prepare your answers in the following areas:

a   reasons for relocation
b   effects of relocation
c   policy of company for European production
d   future in Germany

---

2   Choose a presentation you have given recently and make a list of questions on it. Working with a partner, practise handling the questions.

9 Putting it all together

Objectives

Communication skills	to review what makes a good presentation and to learn to evaluate the effectiveness of a presentation
Language knowledge	a review of delivery techniques and key language points
Presentation practice	to practise giving and evaluating presentations

Communication skills

Pre-viewing

1 Look back at your notes on Unit 1. What problems did Joanna have in that presentation?

2 Read the Video Presentation Context. Imagine you are making the presentation.

    a What will you include in the presentation?
    b How will you prepare for the presentation?

Video Presentation Context

The company	The presenter	The audience	The presentation

Westwood Brewery, based in London, is a traditional company. It has recently created the post of Public Relations (PR) Manager in order to improve the company's image in the market.	Joanna Brookes, the new PR Manager at Westwood Brewery, has organized a meeting to discuss the brewery's corporate image.	The audience of senior managers and outside consultants is expecting a presentation which will clearly introduce the main topics for discussion.	The presentation should provide a clear agenda for the discussion which follows.

Viewing

▶ 3 Watch the video from 29.03 to the end. As you watch, use this assessment form to evaluate Joanna's presentation.

	poor	satisfactory	good	excellent
System				
general organization	☐	☐	☐	☐
introduction	☐	☐	☐	☐
ending	☐	☐	☐	☐
connections	☐	☐	☐	☐
relevance	☐	☐	☐	☐
length	☐	☐	☐	☐
level	☐	☐	☐	☐
Manner				
audience contact	☐	☐	☐	☐
interest	☐	☐	☐	☐
assurance/confidence	☐	☐	☐	☐
Body language				
stance and posture	☐	☐	☐	☐
hands	☐	☐	☐	☐
eye contact	☐	☐	☐	☐
movement	☐	☐	☐	☐
facial expression	☐	☐	☐	☐
appearance	☐	☐	☐	☐
Visual aids				
number	☐	☐	☐	☐
design	☐	☐	☐	☐
relevance	☐	☐	☐	☐
use	☐	☐	☐	☐

Overall impression

▶ 4 Watch the video again from 29.03 to the end. As you watch this time, make notes on the organization of Joanna's presentation. Use this 'classic' presentation structure to help you.

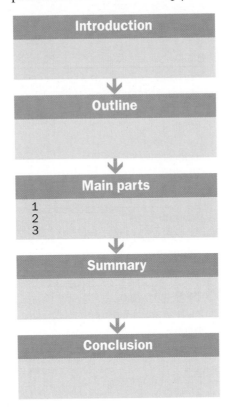

Post-viewing

5 Prepare and give a presentation on a subject you know well. Follow these guidelines and use the assessment form in Viewing 3 to evaluate each other's performances.

Before the presentation

define the audience
clarify the objectives/purpose
plan the content
design suitable visual aids
control the length
follow a clear structure: introduction, main parts, summary and conclusion

During the presentation

keep eye contact with the audience
don't rush (remember to pause)
articulate clearly and project your voice

Language knowledge

JOANNA BROOKES
'One point for discussion, then, is whether we should maintain such different products in our range.'

1 You are going to hear two short extracts from Joanna's presentation again.

  a As you listen to the first extract, mark the linking expressions and the emphasizers/minimizers Joanna uses. Check your answers in the key on page 66.

> The first thing to be said about these products is that they're very diverse. Well, let's take our premium export lager, Hohenbrau. Now this product has always been positioned at the top end of the market. It has a high price and it's only available through selected retail outlets. Altogether, it's quite exclusive.
>
> On the other hand, our Rutter's bitter has an entirely different personality. It's brewed in a traditional way. We put a lot of malt into it, which gives it a rich golden colour. As far as I know, it's always been sold at a medium price, and is available through most supermarkets.
>
> So, as you can see, these are two very different products. One an up-market German-type Pilsener, the other a very English bitter. *One point for discussion, then, is whether we should maintain such different products in our range.*
>
> Let's move on to marketing, and I only want to raise one issue.

  b As you listen to the second extract, mark the pauses and the words Joanna emphasizes. Check your answers in the key on page 67.

> The third element is the people and primarily here I mean the brewery workers and the management. One of the things that shocked me when I first joined Westwood was this organization chart. It's like something from the last century. Do you realize there are ten layers between the shop-floor workers and the Managing Director? In my view, this makes the company slow and unresponsive. I know there are many good things about Westwood, but our image is much the same as it was in, say, the times of Queen Victoria – a very traditional, paternalistic employer. Well, the very least we need to do is discuss whether this image is appropriate for the late 20th century, let alone the 21st.

Language focus Delivery and style

Tempo

Vary the speed – don't talk at the same pace all the time. And pause from time to time – a few seconds of silence are sometimes just as effective as words.

Volume

This is largely a question of voice projection. There is no need to shout. Vary the volume. A quiet part can contrast with a louder part.

Expressiveness

Vary the pitch (high pitch = soprano, low pitch = bass). A good way of varying the pitch is to introduce questions into your presentation. This should force you to raise the pitch a little.

Articulation

The sounds will be clearer if you don't rush your words. If you anticipate difficulty in pronouncing certain key words, practise them beforehand. Usually the problem is the syllable stress.

Sentence length

Avoid reading your text – this should help keep the sentences fairly short.

Register/Style

Make your English sound natural – don't use written English. Decide how formal the language should be for the audience.

Linkers

Use linking expressions to guide the audience through your presentation. Linkers will also help you vary the pace of your presentation.

Emphasizers/Minimizers

It's always a good idea to exaggerate a little – it will help to get your message across persuasively.

2   Use the video transcript on pages 79 and 80 to practise giving Joanna's presentation. Use this assessment form to evaluate each other's delivery techniques. (If possible record your performance and use the recording for feedback.)

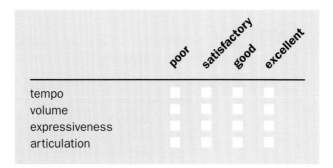

3   Give a short presentation based on the text below. Use this assessment form to evaluate each other's use of language. (If possible, record your performance and use the recording for feedback.)

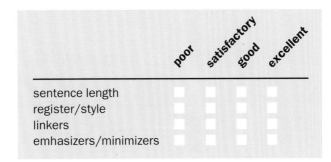

	poor	satisfactory	good	excellent
sentence length	☐	☐	☐	☐
register/style	☐	☐	☐	☐
linkers	☐	☐	☐	☐
emhasizers/minimizers	☐	☐	☐	☐

There are some important things to remember when giving a presentation. One of the key elements, in my opinion, is the contact with the audience. This can be achieved through a variety of techniques. For example, keeping eye contact as much as possible is a very important factor. In fact, if you are speaking to a very large audience, it's a good idea to pick out two or three members of the audience and establish eye contact with them.

Another way of keeping contact is to encourage the audience to interrupt and ask questions during the presentation. This may depend on the time you have allocated but, in principle, it is better to deal with a question at the time it arises rather than later. There are many other factors but eye contact and audience participation will count for 60% success in establishing a strong relationship with your audience.

'It's a good idea to pick out two or three members of the audience and establish eye contact with them.'

Presentation practice

Prepare and give a five-minute presentation on 'The golden rules of presentations'. Evaluate each other's performance using this assessment form.

	poor	satisfactory	good	excellent
System				
general organization	☐	☐	☐	☐
introduction	☐	☐	☐	☐
ending	☐	☐	☐	☐
connections	☐	☐	☐	☐
relevance	☐	☐	☐	☐
length	☐	☐	☐	☐
level	☐	☐	☐	☐
Delivery				
tempo	☐	☐	☐	☐
volume	☐	☐	☐	☐
expressiveness	☐	☐	☐	☐
articulation	☐	☐	☐	☐
Language				
sentence length	☐	☐	☐	☐
register/style	☐	☐	☐	☐
linkers	☐	☐	☐	☐
emphasizers/minimizers	☐	☐	☐	☐
Manner				
audience contact	☐	☐	☐	☐
interest	☐	☐	☐	☐
assurance/confidence	☐	☐	☐	☐
Body language				
stance and posture	☐	☐	☐	☐
hands	☐	☐	☐	☐
eye contact	☐	☐	☐	☐
movement	☐	☐	☐	☐
facial expression	☐	☐	☐	☐
appearance	☐	☐	☐	☐
Visual aids				
number	☐	☐	☐	☐
design	☐	☐	☐	☐
relevance	☐	☐	☐	☐
use	☐	☐	☐	☐

Overall impression

Answer Key

Unit 1 What is the point?

Communication skills 1 *Overall*
Awareness of your audience (Who are they? What are their needs or interests? What do they expect from you?)
Clear objectives (to inform, persuade, welcome, etc.)

System
Planning – have a clear structure and a sense of timing
Organization – have clear connections between the different parts or ideas
Information – make sure what you say is interesting and relevant to your audience
Impact – make sure you have a strong introduction and conclusion

Delivery
Clear, simple, and fluent
Use of natural spoken language
Use of pauses for emphasis

Body language
Use of strong, clear gestures for emphasis
Good eye contact with the audience
Positive, confident, and relaxed manner
No distracting gestures

Visual aids
Clear and simple messsages
Efficient, professional use of equipment

3 *Overall*
She doesn't seem aware of the needs or interests of her audience.
Her objectives are not clear.

System
She is obviously not prepared.
Her presentation is unstructured and confusing.
The information is not organized logically, or linked clearly.
She does not give much useful information.
She has not thought about timing.
There is no strong introduction or conclusion.

Delivery
She hesitates a lot.
She reads from a paper (badly).
She refers to herself negatively.
She uses specialist language.

Body language
Her gestures are not linked to her speech.
She does not maintain eye contact with her audience.
She does not appear confident.
She has some distracting gestures.

Visual aids
She has a screen but does not use it.

Language knowledge

1 a back in 1982 (finished)
   b since that date (unfinished)
   c some time ago (finished)
   d over the last few years (unfinished)
   e now (present)
   f over the same period (unfinished)
   g last year (finished)
   h ten years ago (finished)
   i in 1985 (finished)
   j since then (unfinished)

2 a sold
   b have invested
   c stands
   d have increased
   e retired

3 a back in the eighties
   b at the moment
   c since January
   d last month
   e over the last few years

5 I'd've liked to speak for longer on this subject, but I'm afraid I haven't got enough time. However, I'd* like to say a few words about future prospects. This year, we've had some major problems; next year, we'll face even more severe ones. This is certain, as the market's becoming even more competitive.

   *I would like can be used here for emphasis.

Unit 2   Making a start

Communication skills

4   Geoff only includes a reference to the audience.

5   Geoff includes all the items in the checklist.

Language knowledge

1   Internal presentation: a, d, f, g, i, l
   External presentation: b, c, e, h, j, k

2   a talk about   f finally
   b brief   g questions
   c act as   h go along
   d look at   i hear
   e points of view

3   a 2   e 1
   b 3   f 3
   c 2   g 3
   d 3   h 3

4   a I'm delighted   f sections
   b I take care   g don't hesitate
   c My purpose is   h a chance
   d go through   i in more depth
   e divide

Unit 3   Linking the parts

Communication skills

4   It is not at all clear what Geoff is talking about and there seems to be no organization behind his talk.

5   Point 1: History
   Point 2: Main markets (and Manton news story)
   Point 3: People

Language knowledge

1   a 3   e 5
   b 4   f 2
   c 7   g 6
   d 1

2   a 3   d 1
   b 6   e 2
   c 4   f 5

3 (other answers are possible)
a That was a good meeting. By the way, did I tell you about the match last night?
b Our competitors are becoming stronger. For example/In particular, one of them, Falcon, has a joint venture with a Japanese firm.
c I've divided this into two parts: firstly, the issue of profit-sharing; secondly, the question of share option schemes.
d This year we have lost market share. However, we expect to remain No. 1 in the market.
e There are some vital factors to consider, for example/in particular, the risk of a take-over bid.
f Falcon has reduced its costs by relocating. Similarly, we must consider cutting the cost of our premises.
g We've had a difficult year, but we've still made a healthy profit.
h We expected to lose money in the Far East. In fact/Actually, this was our most profitable market.
i The yen dropped against the dollar. As a result, we made considerable profits on the exchange rate.
j There have been some failures on occasions. However, as a rule, we have been very successful.

Unit 4 The right kind of language

Communication skills

1 *Advantages of reading a presentation*
   - There is little hesitation
   - It may be easier to follow the topic because there are fewer distractions
   - The speaker feels more confident

   Disadvantages of reading a presentation
   - No eye contact with the audience
   - Written English is more complex and often difficult to understand
   - The tone is more impersonal
   - The delivery is less spontaneous
   - The phrasing is less natural, so it's difficult to listen to
   - The reader often speaks too quickly

3 *Version 1*
   Eye contact – no eye contact with the audience
   Language – complex (written), long sentences, few pauses, impersonal
   Manner – closed, uninterested

   Version 2
   Eye contact – good eye contact with audience
   Language – simpler language, shorter sentences, more pauses, more personal
   Manner – open, interested

Language knowledge

1   Spoken language: a, d
       Written language: b, c

2   a   read; distant; prepared; impersonal
     b   spoken; distant; prepared; impersonal
     c   spoken; human; spontaneous; personal

3   a   We discussed the issue of restructuring.
     b   The Finance Manager is directing money into the wrong accounts.
     c   Both companies will sign the agreement later this month.
     d   I have found it rather unreliable.
     e   The press reports that shares are due to rise.

4   a   A reduction in working hours is favoured.
     b   He was forced to resign.
     c   The money has been transferred via the bank.
     d   An autumn sales campaign is being planned.
     e   The new Research Department will be reorganized by Susan.

5

1	d	6	c
2	f	7	a
3	g	8	j
4	i	9	e
5	h	10	b

Presentation practice

1   (other versions are possible)

I'd like to talk today about the costs and benefits of introducing job sharing. What I aim to do is to provide the necessary information for us to make a decision within the next two months. I have divided my talk into the following parts: firstly, we'll look at the financial implications; then, we'll turn to working practices; and finally, we'll look at social effects.

So, let's start with the financial implications. We have carried out a detailed study of personnel and associated costs. And we have seen that, from a payroll point of view, 10% of staff choosing to job share will mean no actual increase in direct salary costs. However, we need to be aware that there will be additional costs in administering salaries.

Unit 5 Visual aids

Communication skills

2 *Design*

Don't use visuals to repeat what you can say with words.
Don't overcrowd visuals with too much information.
Use visuals to support or summarize what you say.
Only use key words, not lines of text.
Think about which kind of visual is right for you
(graph/table/picture/words, etc.).
Use colour (but not too much).

Use

Don't use too many visuals.
Don't read from the visual.
Make sure the audience understands the visual.
Use a pointer and/or masking techniques where appropriate.
Face the audience as much as possible.
Don't block the audience's view.

Remember that your visuals should help you communicate your message.
They should <u>not</u> distract your audience's attention from what you say.

Language knowledge

1

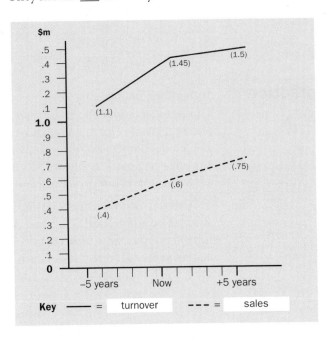

2 a shown/plotted/drawn
   b solid
   c broken/dotted
   d rose/increased/went up

   e fallen/decreased/come down
   f remained constant/stable
   g fall/decrease/drop
   h maintained

3 a has maintained
   b has reduced
   c have raised
   d has held
   e has cut

4 a There has been a slight expansion in the market.
   b There is going to be a dramatic fall in prices.
   c There was a sudden collapse in export sales.
   d There is a steady increase in sales.
   e There has been a gradual drop in salaries.
   f There will certainly be a significant rise in profits.

Unit 6 Body language

Communication skills

1 *Eye contact*
   Maintain good eye contact with different people in the audience.
   Don't just look at one person.

   Facial expression
   Use facial expressions (e.g. smiles) to emphasize your feelings.

   Hands
   Use your hands to emphasize what you say.
   It is safer to keep hands out of pockets – in some cultures this shows disrespect.
   Hold a pen or pointer if you feel more comfortable – but don't play with it.

   Movement
   Don't stand completely still – a little movement between table and board, or between notes and audience, is more interesting.
   Don't move around too much, or the audience may watch you instead of listening to you!

   Posture
   Try to keep your posture upright but relaxed.
   Look straight ahead, not down at the floor or up at the ceiling.

4 *Version 1*
   General appearance: scruffy
   Stance and posture: hunched
   Hands – position: in pockets
   Hands – gestures: no helpful gestures
   Eye contact: none
   Facial expression: depressed
   Movement: static – several nervous gestures

   Version 2
   General appearance: smart
   Stance and posture: upright
   Hands – position: visible and active
   Hands – gestures: clear, helpful gestures
   Eye contact: a lot
   Facial expression: concerned, enthusiastic
   Movement: dynamic

5 a These cost cuts are going to <u>cause considerable</u> pain.
  b We need to draw up a <u>plan of action</u>. I have put <u>some</u> ideas on the <u>board</u>.
  c <u>These</u> are <u>some</u> of the measures we could consider. There are <u>broadly</u> <u>three</u> approaches.
  d <u>First</u>, we could accept the <u>cuts</u> and <u>reduce</u> staff <u>drastically</u>. <u>Secondly</u>, we could <u>fight</u> and <u>hope to achieve</u> <u>some reduction</u> in the level of the cuts. Or <u>thirdly</u>, and <u>this</u> is what <u>I</u> support, we could put forward <u>an alternative</u> proposal. Now, this would…

Language knowledge

1 Emphasize: c, d, e, h
Minimize: a, b, f, g

2 (other answers are possible)
  a This has been an extremely/a very good year.
  b We have had a fairly difficult time/quite a difficult time.
  c We have seen an absolutely/a totally disastrous decline in our profits.
  d It was quite/fairly easy to achieve our objectives.
  e The announcement was completely/totally unexpected.
  f I've got some very/extremely bad news.

3 (other answers are possible)
  a We tend to see things differently. Maybe your experience is a little bit limited.
  b To some extent, you're right. But perhaps we might consider the long-term view.
  c There's just a little bit of time. Perhaps we might discuss this question now.

Presentation practice

1 (other versions are possible)
The trouble with business today is that nobody has any time at all. Companies have drastically reduced their workforces so that far fewer people have to do the same amount of work. To some extent, this means that managers don't see what is happening around them. They need their time to just work through their regular tasks, and they have absolutely no time to take on new initiatives.

Time for reflection is very important. Decisions taken now not only affect today's business, they can also have a significant influence on business in the long term. It seems that strategy is too often the concern of just senior management, when it needs to be the concern of everybody in the company.

Unit 7 Finishing off

Communication skills

1 *The final part of the presentation should include:*
  ■ a clear signal that you are about to end
  ■ a brief, clear summary of what you have said
  ■ a conclusion or recommendation (if appropriate)
  ■ an invitation for questions, to make comments, or start a discussion.

4   *Version 1*
    A signal to end

    Version 2
    A signal to end
    A summary
    A recommendation
    An invitation for questions

5   Signal to end: So, before we move on to discuss ...
    Summary: 3 personnel
    Recommendation: To follow the same order in discussion.
    Invitation for questions: Before we start, are there any questions you'd
                                like to ask?

Language knowledge

1   a The Motivation Presentation
    b The New Idea Presentation
    c The Welcome Presentation
    d The Sales Presentation

2   d, b, c, e, a

3   a 6   d 3
    b 5   e 4
    c 1   f 2

Unit 8   Question time

Communication skills

1   *Handling questions*
    Welcome the question
    Listen carefully to the question – don't interrupt
    Take time to think before you answer
    Check you have understood the question – rephrase or clarify if necessary
    Reply positively – be brief and clear
    Accept criticism positively
    After your answer, check that the questioner is satisfied

Language knowledge

1   a any real future?
    b not such great sales
    c aren't you worried?
    d new products in other areas
    e when will it be ready?
    f ask Tony
    g will it be ready for launch date?
    h yes

2   a 2   d 3
    b 1   e 3
    c 2   f 1

3 **a**

A: Excuse me, could I interrupt?

B: Of course.

A: I'd like to ask you about next year's promotion campaign.

B: Sure, what exactly would you like to know?

A: Well, could you tell me at this stage whether you have fixed a budget?

B: We've got a meeting next week to decide. I'll let you know straight away, if that's OK.

A: Sure, that'll be fine.

b

A: May I ask a question?

B: Go ahead.

A: Would you mind telling us when you're going to retire?

B: Not at all. I'm planning to stop work just after Christmas.

A: Oh good! We'd like to invite you to our Christmas party. Can you come?

B: When is it?

A: It's on the 24th from seven onwards.

B: That sounds fine. I'll look forward to it.

c

A: Are there any questions?

B: Yes, I wonder if you have considered any other options?

A: I'm not sure what you're getting at.

B: Well, you know, other possibilities such as relocating to a cheaper area.

A: I see what you mean. Yes, of course we've looked at all the options and we think this is the best one.

B: But surely relocation would be better for the staff?

A: I'm afraid that's all we have time for now. Perhaps you'd like to talk about that later.

Unit 9   Putting it all together

Language knowledge   **1**   **a**   The *first* thing to be said about these products is that they're *very* diverse. *Well, let's take* our premium export lager, Hohenbrau. Now this product has always been positioned at the top end of the market. It has a high price and it's only available through selected retail outlets. Altogether, it's *quite* exclusive.

On the other hand, our Rutter's bitter has an *entirely* different personality. It's brewed in a traditional way. We put a lot of malt into it, which gives it a rich golden colour. As far as I know, it's always been sold at a medium price and is available through most supermarkets.

So, as you can see, these are two *very* different products. One an up-market German-type Pilsener, the other a *very* English bitter. One point for discussion, then, is whether we should maintain such different products in our range.

Let's move on to marketing, and I only want to raise one issue.

b The *third* element is the *people* / ... and *primarily* here, I mean the *brewery* workers *and* the management. / One of the things that *shocked* me when I *first* joined Westwood was *this* ... / organization chart. It's like something from the *last century*. / Do you *realize* there are *ten layers* between the shopfloor workers and the Managing Director? / In *my* view, this makes the company *slow* and *unresponsive*. / I *know* there are many *good* things about Westwood, / but our image is much the same as it was in, say, the times of *Queen Victoria* – a very *traditional, paternalistic employer*. / Well, the very *least* we need to do is discuss whether this image is *appropriate* for the late 20th century, / *let alone* the 21st.

Tapescript

Unit 1 What is the point?

1 PETER BLAKE

As you all know, the brewery was bought back in 1982 and, as I'm sure you're all aware, there've been some major changes since that date. I'd like to focus on some of these changes and the effect they've had on the way the brewery works.

Some time ago, the new owners announced a new strategy for growth. This strategy had some specific targets – both turnover and profits had to increase a lot. These objectives have led to some very major changes, especially in the areas of production and marketing.

On the production front, we started by reducing the workforce by 5%, but in fact, over the last few years it has dropped further, so that it now stands at just 180, nearly 20% less than ten years ago. Over the same period, we have invested heavily in new plant and equipment. As an indication, last year we spent nearly £1 million on new vats. I'd also like to mention the recent appointment of Geoff Stone, our new Production Manager. He has a wealth of experience in the brewing industry and I think we've already seen the sort of influence he can have on the production side of the business.

I also mentioned marketing. It may surprise you to know that ten years ago Westwood had no marketing department. There was Gordon Peters, the Commercial Director – he's retired now – but otherwise there was no real marketing orientation. In 1985, we recruited Pamela Taylor as Marketing Manager and since then she has built her department into a major force in the company. It's currently active in several areas – notably on the PR front, especially in the local community, and also in sales promotions with a number of recent campaigns in local pubs to promote our beers. Right, I'll stop there. That should help you to understand some of the recent changes at the brewery before we go on to talk about…

Unit 2 Making a start

Language knowledge 1
a My name's Gordon MacNaughton. I'm the new Finance Manager and I hope you won't give me too hard a time!

b Ladies and gentlemen. It's an honour to have the opportunity of addressing such a distinguished audience.

c The subject of my paper today is a critical analysis of the effects of a low carbohydrate diet on…

d I'd like to tell you today about the implications of our recent survey into potential cost savings.

e My aim is to update you on recent research findings and to draw some tentative conclusions.

f This talk should serve as the springboard for a discussion of the benefits and drawbacks of these savings.

g I plan to take only ten minutes of your time this morning.

h During the next half-hour, you will hear about a wide range of research.

i I've divided up my presentation into three parts: firstly, we'll look at the level of savings which we need to make; secondly, I'll run through the options open to us; and, finally, I'll be presenting my recommended course of action.

j The subject can be looked at under two headings: firstly, the definition of this kind of diet; and secondly…

k We have ten minutes allotted for questions following the presentation.

l Feel free to interrupt me at any time.

Internal presentation: a, d, f, g, i, l
External presentation: b, c, e, h, j, k

Unit 3 Linking the parts

Language knowledge 2 a There are some very good reasons for cutting costs. In particular, the fact that we are actually losing money at the moment.

b Now, as a rule, we operate on healthy margins of around 20-25%, but recently we've been forced into aggressive discounting.

c Now, I'm not saying we're the only ones who are suffering. For example, our main competitor, Triton's, has already closed down one of its plants.

d Let's consider the recent point-of-sale competition. The main aim here, by the way, was to raise sales in our major outlets.

e The marketing department launched a new packet size a few months ago. However, sales have hardly taken off at all.

f Both these initiatives have failed. So, in brief, we have been over-hasty in our reactions to the harsher economic climate.

Unit 4 The right kind of language

Language knowledge 2 a The research indicates a failure to recognize the importance of psychological factors on the part of many of our members. It is highly significant that most managers failed to identify this as a critical element in both the making and implementation of decisions.

b It may come as a shock to you to realize that many managers fail to recognize the psychological factor as important. In my view, it is highly significant that we, as a profession, have not really understood how important this factor is in both short-term and long-term success.

c The problem is we've forgotten that our employees are human. We treat them like machines. We give them targets and expect them to get on with it. Where's the caring side of employment gone? I'll tell you where. It's hiding behind a damned set of targets and objectives – that's where it is!

Unit 5   Visual aids

Language knowledge   1   FRANCESCA ROCCA

I thought it would be useful to look at some figures for a moment. Let's start with turnover. As you can see on this graph, I've plotted two lines. The solid one represents the group's turnover, and the broken one the sales generated by our subsidiary in Germany. The figures have been converted into dollars and are shown on this axis in thousands.

OK, let's look at the group's turnover first of all. Five years ago, it stood at $1.1 million. It rose steadily over the following five years and now stands at $1.45 million. Now, we have done some forecasts for the next five years and we anticipate a flattening out at around $1.5 million as price competition becomes more and more fierce.

Fortunately, the figures for our German subsidiary are even better. We started this subsidiary nearly ten years ago. In the early years, growth was gradual and we reached sales of $400,000 five years ago. This represented just under 30% of the group's turnover. Over the last five years, the German market has continued to grow steadily and our turnover is now around $600,000. Unlike our group forecasts, we anticipate some further significant growth and have projected sales of $750,000 in another five years, representing 50% of the group's total turnover. So, as you can see, the German operation is vital to our future.

Unit 6   Body language

Language knowledge   1   a   I think we have to get this into perspective. It's just a minor problem. It's nothing serious.

b   I'd like to make a suggestion. Perhaps we could consider moving our production northwards.

c   I'm afraid we can't get away from it. Our pitifully low quality levels are threatening the future of this company.

d   I've got to say that I've never heard such a ridiculous argument. There is no way we can consider taking this sort of action.

e   There's one more point I'd like to make. It's absolutely essential we make money on this product.

f   We've got a little bit of a problem here. Perhaps it's not central to our business, but I tend to think we should talk about it briefly.

g   In a way, I would say this is quite important. On the other hand, I realize we've got quite a full agenda today.

h   Before we go any further, let me say this has been an extraordinary year, and we've seen some truly remarkable achievements.

Unit 7 Finishing off

Language knowledge 1 a Well, thank you for listening. That brings me to the end of this presentation. Before I leave you to get on with your work, I'd just like to say how glad we are to have you with us, and I wish you a very successful and happy time here at Sinton's. Thank you.

b So, before I stop, let me just run over the key benefits. Firstly, flexibility: it'll work anywhere. We've trialled it extensively and the results are excellent. Secondly, price: as you've seen, it's going to be highly competitive. And lastly, innovation: this is really a breakthrough in the field. Now, I'm sure you've got lots of questions, so fire away.

c So, ladies and gentlemen, that completes my brief introduction. Saville's is a fascinating company, and hopefully you'll get to know us better as you go around the plant. So let me hand you over to Caroline, who's going to be showing you around.

d That brings me to the end of my presentation. I realize that many of you already knew something about our company. Hopefully, I've filled in some of the gaps. As you can see, we've got an impressive display of our products here. Why don't you come and get some hands-on experience?

Unit 8 Question time

Language knowledge 1 SAMANTHA O'NEILL
So that brings me to the end of my presentation. I'd be glad to answer any questions.

QUESTIONER 1
I was interested to hear what you had to say about our medium-range product. Do you think it has any real future?

SAMANTHA O'NEILL
Certainly I do. However, we can't expect the same level of sales as we've generated over the last ten years. Wouldn't you agree?

QUESTIONER 1
I suppose so. It worries me that we don't have any replacements in the pipeline. Doesn't it worry you too?

SAMANTHA O'NEILL
Well, that's difficult to say. It's true we haven't come up with a replacement for the B43. On the other hand, as I pointed out, we have new products in the pipeline in other areas.

QUESTIONER 2
On that subject, I'd like to ask you about the C11 product. Can you tell us how much longer before it's ready for production?

SAMANTHA O'NEILL
That's not really my field. Tony should be able to give you an idea about that.

QUESTIONER 2
Right, I'll talk to him after the meeting.

QUESTIONER 3
Samantha, could I ask you about the production delays on our new A15 product?

SAMANTHA O'NEILL

Please go ahead.

QUESTIONER 3

Well, as you know, we've put together a fairly large-scale advertising campaign. All the space was booked for an October launch…?

SAMANTHA O'NEILL

Don't worry. We'll be ready for the launch date. There are one or two technical problems, but they won't delay us much longer.

QUESTIONER 3

That's good to hear.

2 a May I ask you a question?
 b Do you mind telling me where you got those figures?
 c I suppose you're in town for a week. Is that right?
 d Don't you think we need to take a break?
 e All the job losses are in the plant, aren't they?
 f Could I ask you when you're going to leave?

Unit 9 Putting it all together

Language knowledge

1 JOANNA BROOKES

a The first thing to be said about these products is that they're very diverse. Well, let's take our premium export lager, Hohenbrau. Now this product has always been positioned at the top end of the market. It has a high price and it's only available through selected retail outlets. Altogether, it's quite exclusive.

On the other hand, our Rutter's bitter has an entirely different personality. It's brewed in a traditional way. We put a lot of malt into it which gives it a rich golden colour. As far as I know, it's always been sold at a medium price and is available through most supermarkets.

So, as you can see, these are two very different products. One an up-market German-type Pilsener, the other a very English bitter. One point for discussion then, is whether we should maintain such different products in our range.

Let's move on to marketing, and I only want to raise one issue.

b The third element is the people … and primarily here, I mean the brewery workers and the management. One of the things that shocked me when I first joined Westwood was this … organization chart. It's like something from the last century – do you realize there are ten layers between the shop-floor workers and the Managing Director? In my view, this makes the company slow and unresponsive. I know there are many good things about Westwood, but our image is much the same as it was in, say, the times of Queen Victoria – a very traditional, paternalistic employer.

Well, the very least we need to do is discuss whether this image is appropriate for the late 20th century, let alone the 21st.

Video Transcript

Unit 1 What is the point?

JOANNA BROOKES

I'm sorry I'm a bit late ... um ... I'm not exactly sure how to start this ... um ... I suppose I should start by telling you something about the brewery ... It's old of course, very old, and ... um ... And it was founded in 17, 1778, yes, I think that's right. So it's a very old brewery and ... um ... we use traditional production methods and the products themselves are very, very old ... um ... as you can see, and we have an imperial stout which is very, again very traditional, and it's described as dark, immense, rich with a depth of burnt fruitiness, this beer is an ideal nightcap. Imperial stout is 50% stronger than any of the other beers in the export premium range ... there ... um ... Oh, we also do a lager, we also make a lager which is European, a European type beer and, well, sales have increased a lot over the last year.

Of course, we were a family firm well, in fact, we still are a family firm. As you know the present owner is Ben Westwood ... um ... There was a take-over bid ... um ... I'm not exactly sure when, but it was resisted, and ... um ... we continue to run as a family firm and this is important for the corporate image. Well, in fact this is why we're here today to discuss the corporate image and decide if we, well, it needs to change. We also have horses ... you may have seen them delivering the beer to the local pubs? Yes?

Yes, yes ... um ... production has actually dropped a little over the last few years, although profits have actually held up and that's something we need to discuss ... I mean can we actually continue as a small, independent brewery?

Anyway, that's about it. So ... um ... that is the main question today. So I don't know whether that helps at all, but it's all I can think of really, so I, I'll leave ... I'll leave ... I think that's that, so I'll leave it there, OK?

Unit 2 Making a start

GEOFF MAXWELL

Right, the tour. I've got some overheads here to give you a picture of ... Oh well, never mind, we'll manage without. Anyway, I'll tell you something about the plant we'll be having a look around. I don't know how much you know about us. Perhaps some of you have been here before?

Anyway, I'll start by telling you a bit about the plant so that later you can ... um ... ask questions ... and it should help to understand the process. So, here we are in the main building ...

Version 2

GEOFF MAXWELL

Hello and welcome to Standard Electronics. I'm Geoff Maxwell, the Factory Manager in charge of the plant you'll be seeing today. I know some of you have come a long way today so we aim to make your tour both interesting and worthwhile. Before we start the tour, I'd like to give you a brief presentation about the company – this will help to put the production side of the business into context.

My talk will last about 15 minutes and I'll be using the flip chart. Now there's quite a lot to cover, so I'd be grateful if you'd hold any questions until the end of my talk.

As you can see, I've divided up my presentation into three main parts. Firstly, we'll run briefly through the history of the company. Secondly, I'll tell you something about our main markets – this is important in understanding the production process. And finally, I'll come to the people – our most important asset.

OK? Let's start with the history. Standard started out as a private limited company when it was first established in 1935 ...

Unit 3   Linking the parts

Version 1

GEOFF MAXWELL

In any case, I'll ... um ... I'll tell you something about the plant so that later you can ... ask questions ... and it should help to understand the process ... so, here we are in the main building. Not much of a building. Anyway, we've been based here for more than fifty years, one of the country's best-loved engineering firms. Anyway, it started back in 1943 when there was a need for high quality connections. You know, the sort Britain's famous for.

What we use is a process called pre-priodine electrostatic coating. In this process we apply ...

Version 2

GEOFF MAXWELL

... important in understanding the production process. And finally, I'll come to the people – our most important asset. OK, let's start with the history. Now don't worry! I'm not going to give you a history lesson, just a few key dates. Standard started out as a private limited ...

.. went public. So we've had a pretty eventful 60 years or so. Anyway, I'll leave the history there. If you're interested, you'll find more about Standard in this pretty brochure. You should find one of them amongst all the other bits of paper our PR people love to give out. So, let's turn now to a brief overview of our main markets. If you look at this chart, you'll see our slice of the pie, which in the European ...

By the way, you may have seen the story in the news today about our main competitor, Manton. It seems they're going to bring out a new product which could seriously infringe the copyright ...

So, we'll have to wait and see how the market reacts. Anyway, let me get back to what I was saying about new markets for Standard. I think we have to say that ...

Nobody really knows what the next century will bring. What's for sure is you need people who can adapt quickly. And that brings me to the final part of this short introduction to Standard, and that is to talk about our people. As I said, they are our most important asset. Our total world-wide headcount ...

We've even sponsored a group to sail around Britain. So, before I go on, are there any questions about our personnel policy?

Unit 4   The right kind of language

Version 1

DR LINDEN
The significance of these figures incorporating data from multicentre studies cannot be underestimated. Next slide. In the American part of the survey it was found that success in business can be correlated directly with leadership styles.

An individualistic style appears to be closely associated with rapid career path progression, whereas a group or participative style, despite its evident attractiveness to all members of staff, is correlated with a relatively slow career progression. Next slide. This is further illustrated in my next slide which shows the results of another survey into senior management attitudes.

Although lip service is paid to the concept of participative management, their real perceptions of leadership qualities completely contradict this view. It can be further seen that such surveys ...

Version 2

DR LINDEN
We can't really afford to ignore these results. The survey was one of the most extensive of its kind and covers a wide range of corporations ... We can see in this next slide the results from the American part of the survey. This survey was based on interviews carried out with senior managers in 200 corporations. You can see here ... 35% of the group of managers classified as participative reached senior management positions. On the other hand, 74% of the more individualistic managers achieved senior management status. So, I think the conclusion is self-evident. If you want to reach the top of American companies, you have a much better chance if you adopt a fairly autocratic, top-down approach.

What is important here is not to dismiss the last ten years. Ten years in which the value of participative management has been preached ... No, what we must do is to better understand the motivation of senior management.

If we look at this next slide, we can see the results from another survey into senior management attitudes. This shows how managers firstly evaluate the qualities of a good manager ... and secondly, how they evaluate the qualities of a good leader. What is quite clear is that managers are supposed to be sensitive, adaptable, and cooperative while leaders need to be decisive, dynamic, and single-minded.

So, we find there is a massive contradiction. Good managers are supposed to be participative – to make sure they consult and discuss. Good leaders are supposed to be strong individuals – able to make decisions on their own.

Unit 5   Visual aids

Version 1

JOANNA BROOKES

So, we need to think about the products. Our premium export lager is described as a German-branded Pilsener with an above average alcohol content ... um ... it's positioned at the top end of the market and is only available through selected merchants and retailers.

Anyway, I'm sure you're all familiar with that product ... um ... Our high malt bottled bitter, Rutter's, is described as a traditional West Country bitter with a very dark colour and thick consistency ... um ... It has a high price for a bottled bitter ... um ... and is available through all major supermarket chains and off licences.

As you can see, production in 1984 was around the 245,000 bottles and then during the next five years increased steadily ... Five years ago the annual output reached 480,000 bottles there, as you can see ... and as you can see the figures stayed at that sort of figure until last year when they dipped to 460,000 there, as you can see.

Version 2

JOANNA BROOKES

A very important, perhaps the most important, element in our corporate identity, is our product range. The first thing to be said about this product range is that it's very diverse. Well, let's take our premium export lager, Hohenbrau. Now this product has always been positioned at the top end of the market. It has a very high price, and is only available through specialist retail outlets. Altogether, it's quite exclusive.

On the other hand, our Rutter's bitter has an entirely different personality. It's brewed in a traditional way. We put a lot of malt in it which gives it a rich golden colour. And, as far as I know, it's at a medium price and sold through most supermarkets.

So, as you can see, these are two very different products. One an up-market German-type Pilsener, the other a very English bitter. Our problem is we're no longer sure about what sort of brewery we are ... Anyway, let's leave the products for a moment, and turn to our recent record on the production side.

To make sure we're all in the picture, I've prepared a graph which illustrates our production record over the last twelve years. As you can see, we're only going to be looking at bottled beer production. Now, twelve years ago, we had an annual output of 245,000 bottles – as you can see. Over the next six to seven years, production grew steadily and reached 480,000 way back in 1990. Those were the easy years. It seemed all we had to do was to turn up at work, produce the beer, and the beer would sell itself.

The last five years have been quite different. Production flattened out to around 480,000 for four years, and then, more worryingly, dropped to 460,000 last year. So, this is the background to our meeting today. We can no longer sit back and let the well-established name of Westwood do the work for us ...

Unit 6   Body language

Version 1

DR LINDEN

These cost cuts are going to cause considerable pain. We need to draw up a plan of action. I have put some ideas on the board ... These are some of the measures we could consider. There are broadly three approaches. First, we could accept the cuts and reduce staff drastically ... Secondly, we could fight and hope to achieve some reduction in the level of the cuts. Or thirdly, and this is what I support, we could put forward an alternative proposal. Now, this would mean we have to organize ...

Version 2

DR LINDEN

These cost cuts are going to cause considerable pain. We need to draw up a plan of action. I have put some ideas on the board ... These are some of the measures we could consider. There are broadly three approaches. First, we could accept the cuts and reduce staff drastically. Secondly, we could fight and hope to achieve some reduction in the level of the cuts. Or thirdly, and this is what I support, we could put forward an alternative proposal. Now, this would mean ...

Unit 7   Finishing off

Version 1

JOANNA BROOKES

Yes, yes ... um ... production has actually dropped a little over the last few years, although profits have actually held up ... um ... and that's something we need to discuss ... I mean, can we actually continue as a small independent brewery?

Anyway, that's about it, so ... um ... that is the main question today ... um ... so ... I don't know whether that helps at all, but it's all I can think of really, so I, I'll leave ... I'll leave ... I think that's that ... so ... I'll leave it there, OK?

Version 2

JOANNA BROOKES

So, before we move on to discuss these matters, let me just summarize the main issues as I see them. Firstly, on the product side, there's the question of diversity of product range. Secondly, on the marketing front, we need to review our distribution network. And thirdly, on the personnel side, we need to look at the sort of employer we are, and want to become. So, I suggest we look at things in that order: product, distribution, and people. Hopefully this will help us to agree on a clear way forward. Right, before we start, are there any questions you'd like to ask?

Unit 8 Question time

Version 1

QUESTIONER 1

You seem to have completely ignored the question of male domination of top management posts. Don't you think your results are almost entirely due to the fact that there are practically no women in senior positions in American companies?

DR LINDEN

I did not address the question of gender because it was not my purpose to address it. No doubt it would be interesting to discuss it on another occasion.

QUESTIONER 2

Dr Linden? If you don't mind me asking, could you tell us how the respondents assessed difficult concepts such as individualism?

DR LINDEN

Well it is not important, but if you want to know, just a moment, ... yes, as I thought ... we used the Belbin personality test to position respondents.

QUESTIONER 3

Dr Linden, could I ask you how the surveys were set up? You know, did they use a control group?

DR LINDEN

I believe they used a control group. These weren't my surveys, you know. I can't tell you the details.

Version 2

QUESTIONER 1

You seem to have completely ignored the question of male domination of top management posts. Don't you think your results are almost entirely due to the fact that there are practically no women in senior positions in American companies?

DR LINDEN

I think that's a very interesting point. I'm afraid I didn't have time to address the question of gender itself, because I was mainly concentrating on the question of management style. However, I feel sure that this aspect would be worth discussing at length on another occasion.

Dr Linden? If you don't mind me asking, could you tell us how the respondents assessed difficult concepts such as individualism?

DR LINDEN
Of course. I suppose you're referring to the second survey I mentioned? Well, I'll just check, if I may ... yes ... as I thought, we used the Belbin personality test in order to position respondents. I think that you'll find that this is a fairly standard psychological test with such management surveys. Are there any more questions you would like to ask about the trial?

QUESTIONER 3
Dr Linden, could I ask you how the surveys were set up? You know, did they use a control group?

DR LINDEN
I think I see what you mean. You're interested in the procedure followed for the surveys?

QUESTIONER 3
That's right.

DR LINDEN
I'm afraid that's really outside my field. I myself was not involved in carrying out the surveys. However, I can give you the references afterwards, if they would be helpful.

QUESTIONER 3
Thank you.

Unit 9 Putting it all together

JOANNA BROOKES
Good morning. Some of you may know me better than others, so let me just briefly introduce myself. My name's Joanna Brookes, and I'm in charge of Public Relations for Westwood Brewery. As you may know, this is a relatively new post, and its creation reflects the Board's concern over our position and image in the market. So, one of my first tasks is to define a clear company identity for Westwood, one that will carry us forward into the next century. For this reason, I have asked you all to join me here today to hear your views on a way forward for Westwood. Some of you have been with the brewery for many years, others not at all, so before we start I'd like to outline three main aspects which I see contributing significantly to the brewery's identity.

The first aspect is the products, the second our markets and distribution in particular, and the third key element is our people. So, let's just spend the next few minutes reviewing these three elements ... and please, interrupt me if you have any questions or points you'd like to raise as we go along. So, the products. Arguably, the most important element in our corporate identity is our product range. The first thing to be said about these products is that they're very diverse. Well, let's take our premium export lager, Hohenbrau. Now this product has always been positioned at the top end of the market. It has a high price and it's only available through selected retail outlets. Altogether, it's quite exclusive.

On the other hand, our Rutter's bitter has an entirely different personality. It's brewed in a traditional way. We put a lot of malt into it which gives it a rich golden colour. As far as I know, it's always been sold at a medium price and is available through most supermarkets.

So, as you can see, these are two very different products. One an up-market German-type Pilsener, the other a very English bitter. One point for discussion then, is whether we should maintain such different products in our range.

Let's move on to marketing, and I only want to raise one issue. It's connected with the products really. It seems to me it's going to be very difficult strengthening Westwood's identity in the market when some of our beers are only available through specialist outlets.

QUESTIONER 1
Excuse me, if you don't mind me saying, I think you'll find there are very good reasons for restricting the channels for some of our beers.

JOANNA
That's interesting you should say so and I look forward to hearing more about that in our discussions. Perhaps we can leave it that there are probably very good product reasons why, but that these may conflict with the promotion of the total company image. Would you agree?

QUESTIONER 1
That's certainly true.

JOANNA
So, that covers two of the elements which I think we need to discuss. The third element is the people ... and primarily here, I mean the brewery workers and the management. One of the things that shocked me when I first joined Westwood was this ... organization chart. It's like something from the last century – do you realize there are ten layers between the shop-floor workers and the Managing Director? In my view, this makes the company slow and unresponsive. I know there are many good things about Westwood, but our image is much the same as it was in, say, the times of Queen Victoria – a very traditional, paternalistic employer.

Well, the very least we need to do is discuss whether this image is appropriate for the late 20th century, let alone the 21st. So, before we move on to discuss these matters, let me just summarize the main issues as I see them. Firstly, on the product side, there's the question of diversity of product range. Secondly, on the marketing front, we need to review our distribution network. And thirdly, on the personnel side, we need to look at the sort of employer we are and want to become.

So, I suggest we look at things in that order: product, distribution, and people. Hopefully this will help us to agree on a clear way forward. Right, before we start, are there any questions you'd like to ask?